AT HOME WITH
FLOWERS

⋙ AT HOME WITH ⋘
FLOWERS

THE PRINCIPLES OF FLOWER ARRANGING

Tamaris Ryan

GALLERY BOOKS
An Imprint of W. H. Smith Publishers Inc.
112 Madison Avenue
New York City 10016

With special thanks to my husband, Buck

First published in the United States in 1990 by
Gallery Books, an imprint of W. H. Smith
Publishers, Inc., 112 Madison Avenue, New York,
New York 10016

Project Designer: Stephen Bitti

Designer: Paul Oakley

Project Editor: Carolyn Pyrah

Editor: Susan Dixon

Photographer: Edward Hill

Illustrators: John Woodcock, Michael Woods

Typesetter: Goodfellow & Egan

Studio: The Creative Space

Gallery Books are available for bulk purchase for
sales promotions and premium use. For details
write or telephone the Manager of Special Sales,
W.H. Smith Publishers, Inc., 112 Madison Avenue,
New York, New York 10016. (212) 532-6600.

Printed in Hong Kong for Imago

ISBN 0–8317–0480–2

CONTENTS

INTRODUCTION

FLOWERS HAVE BEEN USED to enhance the home since the ancient Egyptians, Greeks and Romans began adorning their tables with delicate lotus blossoms. They scattered flowers and petals over floors, tables and even beds. During the Renaissance, flowers in vases were used to decorate the interiors of houses and churches. In Tudor England John Parkinson, the herbalist, wrote of '. . . Fresh bowls in every corner and flowers tied upon them and sweet briar, stock, gilly flower, pinks, wallflowers and other sweet flowers in glasses and pots in every window and chimney.' Similarly the Victorians loved to cover every available surface with ornaments, flower arrangements and plants in profusion; this age-old tradition has continued right up to the present day.

The popularity of flower arranging is not hard to explain. The beauty of flowers can be brought indoors, artistically arranged to enhance their natural beauty and to suit them to their setting. Imagine a home full of lovely flowers and the effect they will have on those who live there or who visit it: a colourful, welcoming arrangement on a wooden chest in the hall; an elegant arrangement in the living-room complementing the soft furnishings or a beautiful figurine; in the dining-room a harmonious arrangement toning with both napkins and table-cloth and often providing a talking point at the table; a posy of flowers in a guest's bedroom which reveals a caring touch. From an everyday bunch of simple flowers such as marigolds *(Calendula officinalis)* or anemones *(Anemone coronaria)* to brighten a breakfast table to an extra special arrangement for a birthday, Christmas or summer garden party, some thoughtfully arranged flowers will always lift the occasion.

At Home with Flowers aims to further the pleasure to be gained from flower arranging for both amateurs and experienced alike. Advice about buying and picking flowers and ways of making them last is followed by many inspiring ideas for arrangements to suit individual rooms. There is also a section which includes flower arrangements for special occasions, such as dinner parties, birthdays, Christmas and many more, as well as charts of flowers and foliage commonly used, and when they are available.

A love of flower arranging can easily permeate your life. On a practical level you might find that you are always looking for ways of building up your store of accessories, whether searching in antique shops for containers or unexpectedly finding the perfect vase. A walk in the country or on the beach will never be the same once you have started in earnest. It is essential to carry a plastic bag for any fir cones, stones, driftwood, shells, seaweed and so on for arrangements.

This craft will also enhance your perception. You will find yourself noting the colours and styles of arrangements on pictures of flowers, finding ideas for colour schemes from nature, dress and furnishing fabrics and, of course, from the flowers themselves. Just as an example, look at the purple and yellow face of a pansy *(Viola* spp.), the shades of blue and mauve in a delphinium *(Delphinium* spp.) and the soft pink tones of a rose *(Rosa* spp.) as its petals unfold. I saw a marvellous colour combination in Spain recently: cerise bougainvillea *(Bougainvillea* spp.) and intertwined scarlet geraniums *(Pelargonium* x *hortorum* vars.) tumbling over a wall – what a dramatic colour scheme for a modern home!

I have been arranging flowers for as long as I can remember. There is so much enjoyment to be gained from 'doing the flowers', whether for yourself or for others. I am constantly involved in organizing designs in stately homes, cathedrals and churches. I hope that this book will encourage you to create your own arrangements, thereby beautifying your home with these colourful, fragile objects.

This impressive and colourful arrangement of flowers is both distinctive and lively and softens the brightness of the glass-topped table.

Flowers & foliage:

DARK BLUE STATICE, DARK BLUE IRIS, DARK BLUE MONKSHOOD, PURPLE CLUSTERED BELLFLOWER, CORAL PINK GLADIOLI, CRIMSON AND WHITE STARGAZER LILIES, RED FREESIA, PINK ANTIRRHINUM, WHITE DOUBLE MOCK ORANGE, WHITE FREESIA, WHITE DOUBLE BELLFLOWER, YELLOW IRIS, YELLOW ST. JOHN'S WORT, YELLOW AND WHITE ALSTROEMERIA, WHITE DAISY SPRAY CARNATIONS, LADY FERNS, FLOWERING CURRANT, JEW'S MALLOW (JAPANESE ROSE) LEAVES AND BERRIES OF ST. JOHN'S WORT.

Mechanics:

FLORIST'S FOAM, CHICKEN WIRE, TAPE.

TRICKS
OF THE TRADE

FLOWER ARRANGING IS AN ART. A bold statement you may think, but you will find as you become more competent at arranging a few flowers from the garden, buying others to brighten up your home or admiring a bouquet of flowers received as a gift, that you will also become more creative, truly an artist with flowers.

Naturally you will want to make your flowers last as long as possible to obtain the maximum enjoyment from your creation, so special care should be taken whether you are purchasing from a florist or picking from the garden. There is also a range of treatments for different flowers and foliage before the arrangement is begun and, once completed, its life can be prolonged with satisfactory after-care.

BUYING FLOWERS

Before setting out to buy your flowers give some thought to the style, size and colour scheme of your arrangement and where you intend to place it in your home. Perhaps you are expecting guests for dinner, which will be an intimate candle-lit affair. You have planned to use a white table-cloth, pink napkins and candles and a long, low flower arrangement on the table. In such a setting pale pink spray carnations (*Dianthus* spp.), deeper pink roses and white Singapore orchids (*Orchidaceae dendrobium*) would harmonize with the colour scheme and help set the mood for the evening.

Whenever possible buy the flowers the day before you wish to arrange them, or at least in time for the flowers to have a few hours' drink in water. This preliminary drink helps them last longer when arranged. Select your flowers carefully and ensure that they look fresh and that the foliage is not wilting. Make sure you wrap the flowers for their transport home in order to protect and insulate them from both hot and cold weather.

Once home unwrap the flowers and remove the lower leaves, as these can rot in water and cause bacteria to grow, thereby shortening the flowers' life. Flowers form a seal at the end of their stems when out of water, so it is important to cut about half an inch (1.5 cm) off the ends of

the stems at a slant to break the seal and enable the flowers to absorb water. Place them immediately in a bucket of lukewarm water (this reaches the flower heads more quickly than cold water). Put the bucket in a cool, dimly lit place for a few hours or, better still, overnight, so that the flowers can take up the maximum amount of water before being arranged and placed in a warm room.

Spring flowers are not particularly long-lasting, but daffodils (*Narcissus* hybrids) and irises (*Iris*) will give you several days of pleasure if bought in bud with a little colour showing. Tulips (*Tulipa* hybrids) should not be purchased in very tight bud or they may never open. Spray carnations and chrysanthemums (*Chrysanthemum* spp.) or Peruvian lilies (*Alstroemeria* spp.) and sea lavender (*Limonium [Statice] latifolium*), which have flowers on short side stems, are an economical buy for table arrangements. They also last well, as do Singapore orchids and freesias (*Freesia hybrida* vars). Foliage from various conifers, eucalyptus (*Eucalyptus* spp.) and different types of ferns (e.g. *Adiantum venustrumor* or *Athyrium* spp.) are generally long lasting and will help make your flowers go further.

The flowers require additional treatment to make them last and the hints explained opposite should help to condition the flowers and extend their life.

When you arrive home with bought flowers, remove lower leaves and cut about half an inch (1.5 cm) off the end of the stem at a slant before immersing in water.

STEMS AND FLOWERS REQUIRING SPECIAL TREATMENT

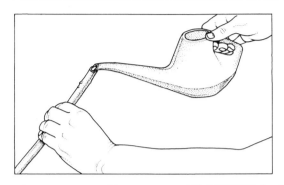

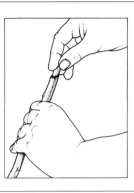

Hollow stems
Suitable for: COW PARSLEY, DELPHINIUMS, LARKSPUR, LUPINS, MONKSHOOD

Use either use boiling water treatment indicated below or fill stem with water, plug end with cotton-wool or foam (which will act as a wick when the flower is placed in the bucket of water), then place stem in deep water.

Young, forced or wilting
Suitable for: AMARANTHUS, BUDDLEIA, DELPHINIUMS, YOUNG FOLIAGE, GERBERA, LARKSPUR, ROSES

Boiling water treatment: pour 2 inches (5 cm) water into a saucepan and bring to boil. Half fill bucket with tepid water. Hold flowers or leaves diagonally and place stem ends in boiling water for 20 seconds. Remove and place in bucket for several hours.

NOTE: Stems are held diagonally so that steam will not affect flowers and leaves. If, however, stems are very short, heads can be protected with a plastic bag secured with an elastic band.

    Although this treatment sounds rather drastic, it is very beneficial and will prevent any wilting — boiling water forces air downwards out of the stem as the water rises upwards, thereby eliminating airlocks, which prevent the water reaching flower heads and tips of foliage.

Hard stems
Suitable for: CHRYSANTHEMUMS, PHLOX, ROSES

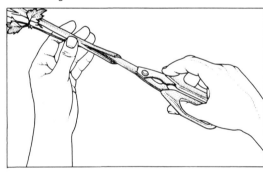

Slit up stem for about 1 inch (2.5 cm) before cutting stem on a slant. Do not hammer stems as this damages them and encourages bacteria.

Woody stems
Suitable for:
FORSYTHIA, HYPERICUMS, LILAC, MOCK ORANGE, PINEBARK

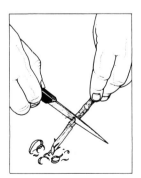

Scrape about 2 inches (5 cm) of bark from stem end, slit stem 2 inches (5 cm) and re-cut on a slant.

Stems which exude latex
Suitable for:

EUPHORBIA, FERNS, POPPIES

Since latex tends to leak from stems, causing flowers to wilt, hold stem end over a candle flame to char latex, make it more permeable and to stop leakage.

Flowering shrubs with many leaves
Suitable for:

BUDDLEIA, LILAC, LOVE-LIES-BLEEDING, MOCK-ORANGE, NICOTIANA, PHLOX, VIBURNUM TINUS

Remove leaves to prevent flowers from wilting. Shrubs also benefit from boiling water treatment described above.

TIPS FOR SPRING FLOWERS

These do not last so well in florist's foam; they prefer shallow water. Cut stems straight across to place on a pinholder (or insert into foam).

Daffodils cut from the garden: wash slime from the cut stems. Rinse them under running water.

Wrap top two-thirds of tulip stems in paper (not transparent wrapping paper) to keep stems straight during conditioning.

PICKING FLOWERS AND FOLIAGE

If you have a large garden it is possible to cultivate a section specifically for flowers for cutting. My own garden is not very large and so I grow bulbs, some perennial plants, flowering shrubs and foliage in various colours plus some variegated leaves. Whether you are able to use a section for growing flowers for cutting or not, you will derive great pleasure from wandering around the garden to select flowers for your arrangements. The best time to cut is in the early morning, as this is the time when plants contain the most water. If this is not possible, cut in the evening as they then contain the most nutrients. Select only the best-looking material for your arrangements.

Sharp secateurs (pruning shears), flower scissors or a knife are the best cutting tools. I always carry a clean bucket containing a few inches of tepid water around the garden so that the cut flowers and leaves can be placed straight into the water. A jam jar will suffice for smaller flowers. Take your bucket full of flowers and foliage inside and condition them in the same way as bought flowers.

BEFORE ARRANGING THE FLOWERS

Just before you arrange your flowers in their container, remove any wilted flower heads or any leaves which may be under water when the flowers and foliage are arranged in the vase. Ensure that the container is clean as dirt encourages bacterial growths which cause the flowers to die more quickly. Also clear glass containers will not show off your flowers to best advantage if they are not gleaming.

Now you are ready to create your flower arrangement.

TIP FOR LARGE LEAVES

Submerge in water for about 30 minutes before conditioning in the usual way.

Suitable for:
Hosta, Bergenia, Arum, Ivy, Fern

AFTER-CARE

Flower arrangements last longest in cool, dimly lit positions. They do not last as well in warm places such as near a radiator, by a sunny window, near an open fire, on top of a television or in a draughty position. In these conditions the water is drawn out of the flowers more quickly, making them wilt.

They also last longer in deep containers or in wide bowls, because the flowers benefit from the humidity surrounding them. Arrangements in small containers need topping up with water every day. A long-spouted watering can works best for this as the water can then be poured slowly into the centre of the arrangements or on top of the block of florist's foam. A light spray with water helps to prolong the life of the flowers, as water is taken up through the petals and leaves as well as through the stems.

The arrangement will also last longer if it is moved to a cooler room overnight.

ADDITIVES TO INCREASE VASE LIFE

There are many ways of prolonging the life of flowers in water – including adding copper pennies or even gin. The reason for adding any substance to the water is to keep it pure and free from bacteria which grow on the stem ends and to reduce the water intake of the plant material. The following additives are most effective:
1 commercial preparations containing a mild disinfectant and nutrients.
2 half a teaspoonful of a very mild disinfectant.
3 half a soluble aspirin to 1 pint (600 ml) water. This will prolong the vase life if there is a large amount of foliage in the arrangement.

Foliage in winter-time
Suitable for:
CUPRESSUS, IVY LEAVES, LAUREL, MAHONIA (OREGON GRAPE), VIBURNUM TINUS

Wash dusty foliage in lukewarm water with a little washing-up liquid (dishwashing soap). It is amazing how this brightens leaves. Foliage can also be soaked in a bath.

Grey foliage, however, does not respond to underwater treatment because of its soft down.

EQUIPMENT AND BASIC TECHNIQUES

When you begin to arrange flowers it is not necessary to rush out and buy all kinds of expensive tools and equipment. There are, however, a few tools that are essential, as indicated below. Further items can be bought later if and when you need them. It is probably a good idea to keep tools in a box (such as one used for fishing tackle) so that they will always be at hand.

CUTTING TOOLS

Scissors
Use a strong pair of sharp scissors to cut the flower stems cleanly. While special flower scissors are not essential, they have serrated blades which will make it easier to cut stems and a small notch at the base of the blade which is useful for cutting wire.

Secateurs or clippers
Use lightweight pruning secateurs (shears) to cut heavier stems and branches, and strong ratchet-type clippers to cut branches up to 1 inch (2.5 cm) thick.

Sharp knife
Use a small sharp kitchen knife to slit woody stems, to scrape 2 inches (5 cm) of bark from woody stems to help the uptake of water and to remove rose thorns.

OTHER USEFUL EQUIPMENT

Deep bucket
A deep florist's bucket with two carrying handles on the rim is particularly useful because it is deep enough to support the flower stems while they are having a drink prior to arranging; additionally, the plant material will not become damaged when lifting the bucket by the two handles (stems can become broken when using an ordinary bucket with a looped handle).

To clean buckets, wash them with detergent and rinse occasionally with a mild disinfectant. Dirty buckets or containers allow bacteria to build up in the water, and this will make the plant material deteriorate more quickly, thereby shortening the vase life of the flowers.

Watering-can
Choose a watering-can with a long spout and a small bore; this is most useful when adding water to an arrangement. The long spout enables you to position the end in the centre of the arrangement and the small bore ensures that the water flows out steadily but not too quickly.

Water spray or mister
Choose a good-quality hand-operated spray. (Cheaper varieties fail to work efficiently after a short while.) The plant material benefits from a light spray because water is absorbed through the petals and leaves as well as being taken up through the stem. Care should be taken not to wet any furniture during this operation; in fact it is probably better to take the arrangement into the kitchen and give it a spray with lukewarm water; as indicated earlier, cold water can give the flowers a nasty shock.

Plastic sheet
Spread a large plastic sheet where you are working to protect the floor from any water spillages, and a smaller sheet on the surface where you are working to protect it from drips and to make it easier to gather up rubbish.

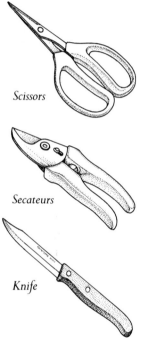

Scissors

Secateurs

Knife

Watering can, deep bucket and water spray

MECHANICS FOR ARRANGEMENTS

This describes the various devices used to hold the stems in position in the containers.

Green plastic foam

Plastic foam, also known as florist's foam, is a green water-absorbent substance sold under various trade names. It may be purchased in a rectangular block or in a cylinder shape. It is an invaluable aid for almost all arrangements.

You can cut dry foam to any shape with a knife. The block should protrude about 1 inch (2.5 cm) above the rim of the container and leave enough space around it for additional water. If you use a shallow container, secure the foam in position by fixing a metal or plastic foam holder to the base of the dry container with florist's fixing clay or modelling clay. Now soak the foam in a bowl of deep water until it sinks and the air bubbles have stopped rising. Press it down on to the pins of the foam holder.

For a small arrangement the foam will probably not require any further fixing; for a large arrangement you should tape the foam to the sides of the container, or tuck a square of 2 inch (5 cm) mesh chicken wire over the block and secure it with tape or string. When the flowers have died, remove the foam and store it in a tightly sealed plastic bag – if the foam dries it will not absorb water again.

USES FOR FLORIST'S FOAM

1 for arrangements in pedestals, candlesticks and any type of raised container which require a flowing downward line.

2 for plant material which needs to flow over the sides in a shallow, flat container, such as an arrangement for the table.

3 for an arrangement which requires transporting, such as a gift; there is less likelihood of the water spilling.

4 for plaques and swags when wrapped in thin plastic sheeting

5 for hanging arrangements without a container. The soaked foam should be wrapped first in plastic sheeting and then in chicken wire.

Dry foam

This foam is coloured brown and is used solely to support dried plant material. Cut and shape with a knife and support in the container in the same way as green foam.

Chicken wire

Before the days of plastic foam chicken wire was the principal support for stems. Today it is often used in vases, low bowls and baskets for casual arrangements and is particularly suitable for soft stems such as anemones (*Anemones* spp.), pansies (*Viola* spp.) and hellebores (*Helleborus* spp.), which are either not happy in foam or are too fine to be supported by a pinholder. The mesh size of the wire should be 2 inches (5 cm).

Form the wire into a loose ball or cone shape and push it down into the container with about 1 inch (2.5 cm) extending above the rim. The wire can be held in place with tape or string and one or two loose ends can be hooked over the edge of the container for extra security. Plastic-covered wire can be rather heavy looking and awkward to use. Take care if using the wire in fine metal or china containers as it may scratch the surface.

Chicken wire can also be used in conjunction with foam, as mentioned above, it can also be used over a pinholder as an extra support for the stems.

Stub wires

These are straight lengths of wire in different thicknesses and lengths, sometimes obtainable in reel form; they may be covered with a fine plastic coating to prevent rust. Their uses are many – you can make false stems for a cone or a preserved leaf with them or splints for a broken dried stem, for example. Bind wires with florist's crêpe tape in a toning colour to keep them in place.

Inserting stub wires up the bent stem of a fresh flower will straighten the stem and help it draw water.

Silver reel wire

This very fine wire is used mainly in floristry work to wire individual flowers and leaves in making up bouquets and wreaths.

Florist's tape and crêpe tape

Use florist's tape to secure the mechanics in the container (right). Use crêpe tape, available in different colour shades, to conceal the wired stems of dried plant material or the stems of fresh flowers used in bouquets and wreaths.

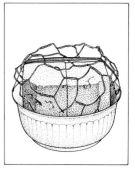

Large arrangements require foam to be fixed securely. Tuck 2 inch (5 cm) chicken wire over block, secure with tape.

Stub wire

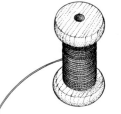

Fine reel wire

Florist's tape

Crêpe tape

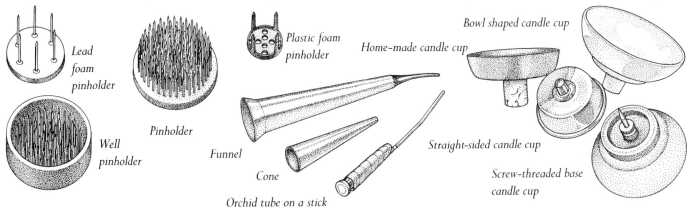

Lead foam pinholder

Well pinholder

Pinholder

Plastic foam pinholder

Funnel

Cone

Home-made candle cup

Bowl shaped candle cup

Straight-sided candle cup

Screw-threaded base candle cup

Orchid tube on a stick

Candle holder

Pinholders (needleholders)

Pinholders consist of a heavy metal base stuck with numerous fine nails or pins. They are normally round and the most useful size for a first purchase is one with a heavy lead base measuring 3 inches (7.5 cm) across. Well pinholders are also available – these are heavy metal containers with either straight or sloping sides with a pinholder fitted into the bottom.

Although pinholders are fairly expensive, they last almost indefinitely with a little care. Straighten the pins out after use and store the pinholder in a dry place to prevent rusting. They are particularly useful both for modern arrangements requiring only a few flowers and leaves and for spring flowers such as anemones and daffodils (*Narcissus* hybrids) which do not last too well in foam. In a large arrangement, heavy plant material can be fixed on the pinholder and be given further support with chicken wire. Fix the dry pinholder on to the dry container with four pellets of florist's fixing clay or modelling clay, taking care not to prick yourself with the pins when pressing the pinholder firmly into position. Insert the stems vertically on to the pins. If you want stems to lean at an angle, insert them vertically initially, then ease into the correct position. To insert very fragile flowers tie small bunches of them with pieces of wool before fixing the stems on the pins. Attach driftwood or candles to the pins of the pinholder by giving them 'legs' of cocktail sticks (toothpicks). Slit fresh woody stems vertically about 1 inch (2.5 cm) from the base to facilitate fixing.

Pinholders can also keep blocks of florist's foam in place and give extra weight to stabilize an arrangement. Foam tends to get stuck in the pins, so place a square of fine nylon over them before placing the dry or wet foam in the container.

Cones and orchid tubes

Cone-shaped water holders come in various sizes. Sometimes they have a 'stem' which may be inserted into the foam, but if the cone does not have one, a stick fixed to the side with florist's tape does just as well. The purpose of a cone is to raise the plant material used. Fill the cone with foam or chicken wire to hold the plant material in place.

Orchid tubes have a small plastic cap incorporating a hole. Fill the tube with water, then insert a single stem. You can tape the tubes on to sticks, which can be inserted in the foam.

Candle cups

These are bowl-shaped or straight-sided containers with a projection which fits into the hollow top of a candlestick in order to convert it into a container. They are available in several different sizes and colours, and are made of metal or plastic. Candle cups enable you to make attractive arrangements in a single candlestick or on a branching candelabra, where the cups can be used in the centre of, say, three out of five branches with candles in the remaining two. Alternatively, place a candle in the centre branch and arrange flowers in candle cups in the outer two. A point worth noting is that if wax has hardened on a candlestick, you can chip it off more easily if you freeze the candlestick first.

Home-made candle cups can be made by gluing a cork to the base of a small shallow tin or lid, which should be painted to tone with the candlestick and to prevent rusting.

Candle cups with screw-threaded bases

These are simple devices which enable you to transform lamps into attractive containers. Remove the bulb and wiring from the lamp and then screw the cup on to the lamp base. Cups are available with internal or external threads.

Tall plant material standing in a jar of glycerine can be supported by placing the jar in a bucket. It also helps bind the stems together.

When immersing leaves in glycerine, place a light weight on top of them to keep them submerged.

PRESERVING PLANT MATERIAL

In the winter-time, when fresh flowers are not so readily available, attractive long-lasting arrangements can be made with preserved flowers, leaves and seed heads. The material is less fragile than fresh plant material; consequently you can spend more time working out and arranging your design because the material will not wilt. It can be used in dark and draughty corners as well as very warm situations, where a fresh arrangement would not survive. Do remember, however, that left in place for too long, the same arrangement can become faded, dusty, sad-looking and lack impact.

METHODS OF PRESERVING

There are several methods of preserving plant material, and the method you choose will depend upon the type of material you wish to preserve.

USING GLYCERINE

Leaves preserved by this method do not retain their natural colour, but will turn into shades of cream, brown and nearly black as the glycerine solution replaces the water in the plant.

SELECTING PLANT MATERIAL

Check that your chosen plant material is suitable for preserving with glycerine. *See* the Directory of Flowers and Foliage on pages 46–51.

In general, choose mature foliage; do not use leaves which are too young or those which have begun to turn colour in autumn, and always select leaves and sprays which are in good condition and are well shaped. Remove the lower leaves and any dead or damaged leaves. Trim away surplus twigs and leaves to obtain a good shape.

Method 1 (standing method)

The glycerine solution consists of one part glycerine and two parts very hot water.

1 pour the glycerine solution into a large instant coffee jar to about 2 inches (5 cm) in depth. Stand a metal spoon in the jar (to prevent the jar from cracking when the hot water is added), then add twice as much very hot water as glycerine, and stir well. Do not let the level of the solution fall too low during the preserving process (which takes about 4–10 days), but fill up as necessary.

2 before putting the stems into the solution re-cut the ends on a slant and slit the stems vertically for about 1 inch (2.5 cm); this enables the plant to take up the liquid easily.

3 if the jar contains tall stems, stand it in a bucket to prevent the jar from falling over; it also helps to bind the stems together.

4 you can leave the stems in the solution until the leaves have changed colour but if you leave them in too long, the glycerine sometimes oozes out of the leaves. Moreover, the plant material tends to go mouldy if kept in a damp place. The best guide is to feel the topmost leaves and stems; if they feel oily the glycerine has been fully absorbed and the stems can be removed.

5 hang the stems upside-down to allow the glycerine to permeate the plant.

6 strain and retain the remaining solution to use for filling up.

Method 2 (immersion in glycerine)

1 prepare the glycerine and water mix as described in Method 1.

2 lay the leaves in a shallow non-metallic dish and pour the mixture over the leaves, ensuring that they are completely covered. A more satisfactory result is obtained if the dish is not overfilled with leaves.

3 place a light weight on top of the leaves in order to keep them submerged. It can take several weeks to preserve leaves by this method; check them occasionally to see if they have absorbed the glycerine.

4 when ready, remove the leaves and wash them in lukewarm water containing a drop of washing-up liquid (dishwashing soap). Rinse in clear water and dry with absorbent paper towels.

AIR DRYING

Check that your chosen plant is suitable for air drying. *See* the Directory of Flowers and Foliage on pages 46–51.

SELECTING PLANT MATERIAL

In general, pick plant material with as long a stem as possible on a dry day. This will enable the plants to dry more quickly and retain a good colour. Select plants which are undamaged and have a good shape and pick flowers just before they are fully developed. Pick seed heads while they are still green; they will then be in a better condition than those which are left to mature on the plant. Gather wheat (*Triticum* spp.) and grasses when green to retain some of the colour when dried. Remove all leaves as these do not dry successfully.

Method 1 (hanging)

1 wire thin stems or replace the natural stem with a stub wire if the stems are very fragile.

2 gather the stems into small bunches with heads at different levels, slip a soft rubber band over the ends and then tie with wool or string, leaving long ends to hang the bunch. The rubber band is useful to grip the stems, as they will shrink while they are drying.

3 hang the well-separated bunches upside-down to keep the stems straight and enable the sap to run down, hence keeping the stems under the head strong while drying takes place.

4 place the bunches in a dry, airy place and, if possible, in the dark for the best colour retention. They should be left hanging until the plant material is crisp to the touch. This will generally take between one and six weeks.

Method 2 (in water)

This may seem like a contradiction in terms, but there are some flowers which require this treatment.

1 re-cut the flower stems on a slant, then stand them in a glass jar containing ½ inch (1.5 cm) of warm water. Alternatively, make an arrangement in a vase containing the warm water.

2 leave in position until the flowers feel papery and have absorbed all the water. This will happen slowly.

Method 3 (using newspaper)

Bracken (*Pteridium aquilinum*), ferns (*Adiantum* spp.) and grasses can be dried between sheets of newspaper.

1 lay the bracken in a single layer on two sheets of newspaper, cover with two more sheets of paper, then a layer of bracken and so on.

2 place the pile of bracken and papers under a bed or in a dry place where they will not be trodden on. The plant material will dry with some natural curves and will look much more attractive than if pressed flat under the carpet.

PRESSING

This prevents the plant material from curling up and becoming shrivelled. On completion of the drying process the plant material will, however, be very flat. For best results, three pressing methods are given: choose the one most suitable for your plant material.

SELECTING PLANT MATERIAL

Check that your chosen plant material is suitable for pressing. *See* the Directory of Flowers and Foliage on pages 46–51. In general, do not choose flowers with a hard, thick centre, or very thick or succulent material. Fine, thin material is only suitable for pressed flower pictures; use more robust material in arrangements. A false stem made from a stub wire can be fixed prior to drying the plant material.

Method 1 (using flower press)

1 press thin, delicate flowers and leaves between sheets of blotting paper in a flower press or between the pages of a telephone directory.

2 ensure that the plant material is well spaced out and does not overlap.

3 use tabs to indicate what type of material is in between the pages.

4 the longer the material can remain in the press, the better the colour retention. It should

This dried arrangement picks out the colours of the painting above it.

Flowers & foliage:

PINK AND CREAM LARKSPUR, WHITE, CRIMSON AND MAUVE SEA LAVENDER, CRIMSON LOVE-LIES-BLEEDING, RED ROSES, PALE GREEN LADY'S MANTLE, PALE GREEN HYDRANGEAS, DYED-RED PEARLY EVERLASTING, BEIGE LOVE-IN-A-MIST SEED HEADS.

Mechanics: DRY FLORIST'S FOAM.

remain in the press for at least three months, but it can be left for up to a year for pressed flower pictures.

Method 2 (using newspaper)

1 press heavier plant material between sheets of newspaper.

2 place under a heavy book and leave somewhere out of the way for at least 3 months.

Method 3 (ironing)

1 place large, flat leaves between sheets of newspaper or brown wrapping paper.

2 press with a domestic iron on the 'wool' setting.

3 keep the leaves in between the sheets of paper and place under a carpet for about a week to complete the drying process.

USING DESICCANTS

Preserving flowers with desiccant crystals enables the natural form and colouring of the flower to be maintained; the flowers will, however, be extremely fragile and will need care in handling and storage.

SELECTING PLANT MATERIAL

Check that your chosen plant material is suitable for preserving in desiccant crystals. *See* the Directory of Flowers and Foliage on pages 46–51. In general, dry only a few flowers at a time; select only perfect specimens and pick the flowers on a dry day.

Method 1 (traditional)

1 purchase either alum or borax from a hardware shop or silica gel crystals and special desiccants by mail order. Borax is suitable only for small or white flowers as the powder is difficult to remove.

Collect the following equipment: an airtight tin or plastic box large enough to contain the flower and desiccant, sticky tape to seal the box, stub wires, a fine paintbrush and a knitting needle or skewer.

2 pick the flower, and cut the stem, leaving about 1 inch (2.5 cm).

3 make a false stem by pushing a stub wire up the natural stem or attach it with crêpe tape.

4 coil the wire around so the flower takes up less space.

5 pour a 1 inch (2.5 cm) layer of the desiccant into the box and place the flower on the crystals.

6 sift more desiccant over the flower.

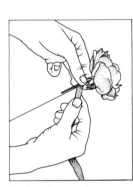

1 *Attaching stub wire with crêpe tape to make a false stem.*

2 *Sifting desiccant over the flower to preserve it.*

7 use the needle to move the petals, ensuring that the flower retains its original shape.

8 shake the box very gently to ensure the desiccant fills every crevice. The flower should be covered with at least ½ inch (1.5 cm) desiccant.

9 seal the lid with sticky tape and label it with the type of flower and the date.

10 when the drying process is finished the flower should feel dry and papery. Finer flowers take less time to dry than thicker ones; experience will dictate how long it takes.

Method 2 (using a microwave oven)

This method of preserving the plant material is the same as the desiccant method above with one important exception: metal must NOT be used for wiring or for a container.

1 place the box in the oven for about 2½ minutes for a small rose.

2 leave it to cool before removing the flower.

3 flowers preserved by the dessicant method can be made more durable by spraying with a special commercial finish or a matt acrylic coating for paper.

METHODS OF STORAGE

Dried plant material is usually fragile and should be stored carefully in closed cardboard boxes or hung in bunches. Store the boxes in a dry place as damp conditions cause plant material to deteriorate and it may become mouldy.

Clean dusty glycerined plant material by washing it in lukewarm water containing a few drops of washing-up liquid (dishwashing soap). Rinse in clear water and allow to dry thoroughly before re-using or storing.

If the plant material becomes flattened or out of shape during storage, hold for a few moments in the steam from a kettle; this will soften it and it can then be gently eased back into its original shape. Ensure that it is thoroughly dry before storing it again. (Do not use for material preserved in desiccants.)

Place plant material dried with desiccants in a storage box sprinkled with a few desiccant crystals. Support the flowers with tissue paper or push the wire stems into a block of florist's foam in a deep box. In both cases keep the box covered.

Note: Do not store the material in plastic bags as condensation will cause dampness and consequent mould.

MECHANICS

Stems can be supported either in dry florist's foam, on a pinholder or in modelling clay, or as a permanent arrangement in either plaster of Paris or self-hardening clay. They can also be supported by 2 inch (5 cm) mesh chicken wire crumpled loosely into a vase without water. If you wish to use dried materials in water or wet florist's foam, seal the stems with candle wax, varnish or nail polish to prevent them from becoming soggy. Seal glycerined material as above when using in water to prevent mould from forming.

Secure the mechanics for preserved plant material firmly in the container because the material is very lightweight and the arrangement could tip over in a draught. A heavy foam holder taped to the sides of the container will be helpful, as also will a cap of chicken wire secured with tape or string and covering the foam – for heavier plant material. Push the material well down on to the pins of a pinholder or insert firmly into florist's foam. A heavy container or the extra weight of a large pinholder covered in fine nylon and placed under the foam will give additional stability.

An arrangement composed entirely of preserved plant material requires no water. It is possible to use plant material preserved by the glycerine method together with silk flowers or fresh flowers and foliage.

Thin, fine pressed material is not suitable for arrangements as it is too delicate. It can be fixed to a backing with adhesive and used for pictures, greetings cards and plaques.

Heavier plant material can, however, be used for arrangements. You might need to strengthen the stems with a stub wire bound with tape; alternatively, use a false stem of wire or a thick stick. Stems can also be lengthened with a stub wire or stick bound with tape.

Flowers dried with desiccants look very pretty when arranged with other preserved material as the colour is maintained. Remember, however, that they are very fragile and cannot be arranged in water or wet florist's foam. They can also be used to make attractive pictures. A deep box-type frame will be necessary so that the glass does not flatten the flowers. Plaques, swags (see page 102) and garlands are other uses for desiccant-dried flowers.

BASES

These are an important part of flower arranging. Not only do bases protect the furniture on which the container stands but they can add a harmonious or contrasting colour and visual balance to an arrangement.

It is important to choose the right type of base for a particular flower arrangement; for example, a velvet-covered base will complement a traditional arrangement in a porcelain container, an unpolished slice of wood looks right used as a base for a naturalistic landscape-type design and a hessian-covered board can tone with the texture of a rough pottery container. The thickness and size of a base will also affect both the scale and visual balance of an arrangement: a base used under a tiny arrangement should be small enough to be in scale with the container used yet thin enough to ensure that the design is not given a bottom-heavy look.

DIFFERENT TYPES OF BASES

Covered boards
Cake boards, hardboard or special boards cut to ¼ inch (0.5 cm) thickness can be cut to shape and covered with fabric as follows:
1 place the board down on the material and cut around the material about 1 inch (2.5 cm) wider than the width of the board.
2 rub stick glue suitable for fabric and cardboard or wood all around the outer edge of the board to a depth of about 1 inch (2.5 cm).
3 bring the material up over the edge and press down firmly, ensuring there are no creases around the outer edge of the board – see diagram, above right.
4 place the board under a heavy book while the glue is drying.
5 turn the board over to the wrong side and snip off the folds of material with sharp scissors – see diagram, below right.
6 stick self-adhesive baize or strong paper on the back of the board to finish.

Wooden bases
A cross-cut slice of a branch about ½ inch (1.5 cm) thick makes an excellent base for an informal design. These can be purchased ready cut, usually varnished on one side and left natural on the other. D-I-Y stores and timber merchants will generally cut wood or board to a pattern supplied by yourself.

1 *Covering a board with fabric to make a base and glueing the underside.*

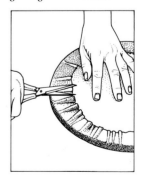

2 *Snipping off the folds of material with scissors.*

17

ACCESSORIES

Anything which is used as part of or placed beside a flower arrangement and is not made of plant material is referred to as an accessory. Many objects in the home can be used, such as a figurine, a group of shells or perhaps an old coffee pot, all of which will look attractive with a complementary flower arrangement. Imagine a bronze figurine on a toning velvet base surrounded by glowing red flowers and lime green foliage and with a few darker flowers or foliage to pick up the colour of the figurine.

An accessory can either be incorporated into an arrangement or stand beside it. Place it in position before beginning the arrangement so that it does not look like an afterthought. If you are worried about knocking it over as you work, place it in position and arrange the first few pieces of plant material to get an idea of the outline of the arrangement. Remove the accessory and then replace it when the arrangement is almost completed, making any necessary adjustments.

When you first use an accessory in conjunction with flowers you may well misjudge the size relationship or scale; very often a small accessory is lost in a mass of flowers. A design which includes a dainty figurine is one of the most difficult to compose correctly; the relationship between the size of the figurine and the flowers can be disproportionate and the volume of plant material used is often not in scale. For example, a 6 inch (15 cm) tall Dresden china lady needs small, pretty flowers such as freesias (*Freesia* x *hybrida* vars.), spray carnations (*Dianthus* spp.), dainty gypsophila (*Gypsophila* spp.) and tiny roses (*Rosa* spp.) to complement its size, colour, texture and elegance. Alternatively, a weighty-looking sculptured bust requires larger, bolder flowers like gerberas (*Gerbera jamesonii*) or lilies (*Lilium* spp.).

It is important that the style of an accessory suits its setting as well as its accompanying flower arrangement. The dainty Dresden figurine would look out of place in a modern, black-and-white painted hall. A smooth-polished, slender wooden figure with gerberas, however, could look wonderful in this setting.

In short, all the components of the design – flowers, container, base and accessory – need to harmonize in scale, style, suitability, colour and texture.

Opposite: this Oriental-influenced design uses the willow mirror to reflect the dramatic shapes of flowers and accessories. Its design and colour scheme are taken from the chest on which it stands.

Flowers & foliage:
RED PAINTER'S PALETTE (FLAMINGO LILY), GREEN FATSIA LEAF, BLACK PAINTED WILLOW BRANCHES.

Mechanics:
ELASTIC BAND TO HOLD FLOWERS.

CONTAINERS

These incorporate any receptacle that will hold water or which can be adapted to hold water. You probably already own various jugs, pottery ovenware, baskets, shallow bowls, ashtrays, shells and so on.

One of the most useful containers is a round pottery dish with a narrow neck; it can be used for a tallish modern arrangement, a long, low table arrangement, a posy style or a medium-sized traditional triangular arrangement. A wide, shallow bowl, a tall, narrow cylinder, an urn or a bowl shape on a stem are also useful. The latter can be constructed from a candlestick with a candle cup inserted in the top.

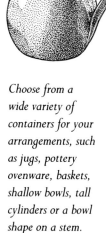

Choose from a wide variety of containers for your arrangements, such as jugs, pottery ovenware, baskets, shallow bowls, tall cylinders or a bowl shape on a stem.

More unusual containers might include large shells, dramatic modern containers, miniature or hand-blown glass vases, a wicker hamper, handwoven basket or wooden jewel box.

Before buying, consider the position in which the container is most likely to stand in your home, the colour and style of the room and the size of arrangement you wish to create. Containers in a fairly neutral colour will adapt to a greater variety of colour schemes and will tend to show flowers to best advantage because the receptacle is less dominant in hue. The colours of dark leaves, greyish stone, bracken in autumn, and greenish-brown bark complement most plant material well.

Line non-water-resistant containers such as basketware, marble, alabaster or onyx with a plastic bowl. Clean alabaster with a soft cloth dipped in olive oil; sponge onyx carefully with methylated spirits. It is also a good idea to line precious silver or other metal containers with the right-sized plastic bowl to prevent them from becoming scratched. Silver rose bowls, sugar bowls and bon-bon dishes make unusual and distinctive containers.

Plastic containers are inexpensive and can be purchased in many shapes; the colours are, however, sometimes not very subtle but you can paint them in a variety of colours to suit an arrangement.

When you have gathered a collection of basic containers, search out the more unusual ones, such as large shells, an antique copper coffee pot, an unusual tiny vase to hold a posy of spring flowers, a dramatic modern container or a handwoven basket purchased on a trip abroad. Alternatively, antique wooden jewel boxes, wicker hampers and baskets and small metal or lacquered boxes all make delightful containers when lined with a plastic bowl filled with florist's foam.

To clean cut-glass vases, jugs or decanters, soak them overnight in a solution of denture cleaner; household bleach and water; water and torn-up pieces of newspaper; or a solution of 2 tablespoons (30 ml) vinegar to a vase of water. In the morning rinse and dry the glass. Fine china vases should never be washed in detergent as it may cause the colours to fade; use lukewarm soapy water, and rinse with cold water.

DRIFTWOOD

Driftwood used in flower arranging can include bark, roots or branches from woodlands and hedgerows or wood found on the seashore and sculpted by the sea. Driftwood should be a feature of the arrangement and not hidden behind the flowers and leaves. Used as a semi-permanent outline, it can be left in position in the container, renewing the flowers as necessary.

You can use a striking piece to give height and dramatic effect to a modern design incorporating bold flowers and leaves at the base. Slender branches or roots can supply the correct height for an arrangement in a particular setting. This is particularly effective in the spring with short-stemmed bulb flowers and a branch of driftwood representing the bare-leafed trees. It can also give height to a *pot et fleur*; these arrangements of house-plants and cut flowers sometimes look bottom-heavy, and the tall driftwood helps give better visual balance.

Heavy pieces of wood with interesting shapes often have a natural hollow which can be enlarged or reshaped to hold a container filled with water. The wood must stand steadily to avoid water spillages. Polished and stained driftwood can give a very sophisticated effect, or leave it unpolished for naturalistic designs.

When cleaned and lightly polished or left in its natural state, naturally sculpted driftwood can make an attractive feature in a room. It can look very dramatic if you place it on a harmonious base and complement it with a few striking flowers and leaves in a concealed container. Small, flat pieces of wood or bark are very useful for concealing mechanics.

SELECTING AND PREPARING DRIFTWOOD

Unless you are purchasing ready-cleaned and prepared driftwood, look for wood that is hard and has an interesting shape. It is, of course, possible to remove small projections, but if you try to remove large ones you may spoil the natural look of the driftwood. Leave any wood that is soft, rotten or worm-infested; it will only continue to deteriorate.

Fill a bowl big enough to contain the wood with warm water, detergent and some disinfectant or bleach. This will clean the wood and kill any small insects which may be lurking in the crevices. Scrub the wood, rinse and allow to dry in the sunshine or in a warm place in the house. After drying, remove any soft wood with a pointed knife or chisel and clean the wood with a wire brush. Do not scrub or brush grey wood as this will remove the grey sheen.

Remove any small twigs with secateurs (pruning shears) and use a small pruning saw for larger pieces. Avoid altering the wood too much or it may then lose its natural look.

Colouring
Paint the wood with gloss or matt paint if the natural colour is not required. Blacken it, if necessary, either with matt black paint or black shoe polish. You can highlight wood for use at Christmas time with gold, copper or silver paint.

As wood stain, linseed oil and different-coloured shoe polishes will darken and alter the colour of the wood, try them out first on a part of the wood which will not be visible once the arrangement is complete.

Polishing
Colourless furniture wax or shoe polish will give the wood a soft shine. Apply the wax or polish generously with a soft brush or cloth, leave to soak in for 24 hours, then brush the wood to bring up the shine, finishing by polishing with a duster. If a stronger shine is required, repeat the process.

Varnishing
In order to protect the wood from water you can paint it with a colourless matt varnish. Do not, however, varnish or polish grey wood as the greyness will disappear.

MECHANICS

Having prepared your piece of driftwood you will have to support it for use in a flower arrangement. There are several ways of doing this, as follows:

1 saw a slice from the bottom of a large piece of wood. For a straight line, dip the wood in a jug or bowl of water and hold it at the angle you wish it to stand, then saw along the resulting tidemark. The wood can then stand on its own.

2 a wedge screwed and glued to the wood to hold it level will make it unnecessary to saw the wood. Use dowel as a false leg or legs. Drill a hole in the wood the same diameter as the dowel and glue it in position. Do not cut the dowel until you are sure of the length required.

3 fix a well-balanced piece of driftwood to a slice of wood by screwing upwards through the base with a countersunk screw. It is important to use a screw as nails may split the wood. The base will then be a permanent fixture.

4 fix lightweight, slender branches on a pinholder or push firmly into florist's foam.

5 purchase a lead base with a central screw and clamps fixed to an inverted pinholder to support lightweight wood.

6 use plaster to fix the wood permanently to a base or container. Carefully support the wood in the desired position in the mound of plaster while it sets.

To level a piece of driftwood for an arrangement, dip it in water, hold it at the angle you wish it to stand and saw along the resulting tidemark.

DESIGN

*F*LOWER ARRANGING will open your eyes to the world around you and you will probably gain inspiration from many sources. Flower arrangements from the past are depicted in many superb Dutch flower paintings, wood carvings by Grinling Gibbons, sculpted stone flowers, old patterned vases and even in the written word or a song, to give just a few examples.

Other inspirational starting points might be the subtle colours of a Gainsborough painting, the textured patterns of embroidery and weaving or the sinuous curves of a sculpted figure. The world of nature itself is another invaluable source. Imagine the lacy branches of a tree silhouetted against a winter sky, the glorious colours of a flaming sunset and the many shades of green in your own garden. Containers can also inspire the arranger: imagine a simple arrangement of lilies (*Lilium* spp.) in a tall and elegant vase or simply daffodils (*Narcissus* hybrids) from a spring garden arranged with a few twigs and leaves in a pottery container will most certainly brighten any dull corner. If you keep looking you will be surprised at the range and variety of creative stimuli.

Carving by Grinling Gibbons in Trinity College Library, Cambridge. The same elements of design exist in this carving as in a flower arrangement, and the same principles have been applied to create a harmonious form.

DESIGN CONSIDERATIONS

Consider what are generally known as the Elements of Design. These consist of form or shape, line, space, colour and texture. Some or all of these elements exist in natural plant material as well as in artists' materials such as paint, stone, wood or woollen threads.

The ways in which these elements are combined to create a finished flower arrangement are called the Principles of Design. These are scale, proportion, balance, rhythm, lighting, contrast and variety, dominance or emphasis and harmony.

Here the driftwood container forms a basic feature of the total arrangement. A harmonious effect is created by the balanced use of colour and contrasting textures.

Flowers & foliage: YELLOW DAFFODILS, SILKY GREY CATKINS OF FASCIATED WILLOW, MOTTLED GREEN ITALIAN ARUM, DRIFTWOOD, BRACKET FUNGI.

Mechanics: TWO WELL PINHOLDERS.

Once you have grasped the design concepts you will be ready to consider the style of arrangement best suited to your needs and décor. You can then begin constructing an arrangement to form a focal point within a particular room.

THE ELEMENTS OF DESIGN

Flowers and leaves with all their colour, texture and shapes are the living material with which special effects are created. You will need to think about the design of your arrangement when picking or buying the flowers and leaves: colours which will blend together well, shapes which will complement one another and textures to give further interest. Try to visualize the whole arrangement and its position in your home while you are selecting your plant material. In this way you will be able to pick the right colours, shapes and textures much more quickly. You will also be better able to select just the right amount of material for your needs – too much is uneconomical and too little is infuriating.

SHAPE OR FORM

When looking at a flower arrangement the eye concentrates first on the whole shape of the design and then on the various shapes of the plant material included in the arrangement. There are many beautiful shapes in plant material: just think of lilies, roses or daffodils. The shape may be exciting, such as a bird-of-paradise flower (*Strelitzia reginae*), or a painter's palette, or flamingo lily (*Anthurium andreanum*), or bold, such as a bergenia (*Bergenia* spp.) leaf or a large-headed dahlia – the variety is infinite. Plant material is three-dimensional, having both width, depth and height, the exception to this being some foliage which is almost flat. The completed arrangement also has these three dimensions.

Form may be regular or irregular, symmetrical or asymmetrical, angular or curved, and both the individual parts and the design as a whole have shape and form. Some repetition of shapes and variety of form within the design give the most pleasing effect.

The basic shape or form of an arrangement lends mood or character to the design. A low arrangement in a rectangular container induces a sense of stability, while a pyramid or triangular arrangement with its wide base seems secure, particularly in a low, bowl-shaped container. Tall, slender cones suggest aspiration or upward movement, and curved or spherical forms imply life, growth and gentle movement.

Traditional designs in flower arrangement tend to have gradual impact. Shapes within the design are mainly rounds and transitional forms.

Modern designs are much more dynamic than traditional ones; they have impact and quick movement and therefore use mainly rounds and lines which cause the eye to move rapidly over the arrangement.

LINE

This is an expressive element, giving movement and rhythm to a design. A gentle curve suggests a slow movement, a straight line speeds the eye along, a zigzag gives a jerky feeling, while a thick horizontal line gives stability to an arrangement, particularly when a container or base takes this line.

Line may involve the shape of the whole design, whether vertical (tall), triangular, horizontal (such as in a low dining-table arrangement), S-shaped (Hogarth), dome-shaped, crescent-shaped or asymmetrical. Lines within a design also give direction: in a traditional arrangement the plant material forms lines radiating out from the focal point. Stepped lines of colour within a symmetrical arrangement will create impact and give movement to a static design. Linear traditional designs, for example those which are S-shaped, vertical, diagonal and crescent-shaped, require less plant material than other traditional arrangements, like the symmetrical triangle. In all of these designs the

Vertical

Crescent

S-shaped

Horizontal

largest flower is placed at the centre of interest, while the remaining plant material decreases in size towards the outer points, so that the eye easily follows the line of the design.

Modern designs use the minimum of plant material and line is always the dominant feature; sparse designs must make good use of space within the arrangement. In restrained modern designs line is used simply to create effects: strong vertical lines to give an uplifting feeling, crossing and zigzag lines to create drama and diagonal lines to produce exciting movement.

Direct lines
These are strong and plainly visible, often created by the lines of individual branches or flowers and used chiefly in modern designs. Bare branches, iris leaves and gladioli (*Gladiolus* spp.) flowers are good examples.

Indirect or broken line
This is formed by a row of rounds or other shapes. The eye follows a continuous line which visually joins the rounds and gaps between them. A line of almost equally spaced flowers will create this effect.

Line by the use of repetition
Imagine a line of poplar (*Populus* spp.) trees or the individual leaves forming a mahonia leaf; in each case the shapes of the trees and the leaves carry the eye in a directional line because the tree and leaf shapes are repeated.

Outline
The outline forms the outer boundary of a shape or that of the whole design, for example the outline of a traditional design could be a triangle.

(Modern designs do not have a clearly defined or geometrically shaped outline.)

Lines of continuance
In order to give a design rhythmical movement the eye needs to move throughout the arrangement along lines of continuance. These are invisible paths which the eye follows right through the arrangement in a good design. The eye is attracted to round shapes, bright colours and shiny textures. Consequently these are the most dominant features and less dominant ones are needed to move the eye on to other parts of the design along invisible paths.

Lines to create mood or feeling
Lines can help to give a mood or special feeling to a flower arrangement. Gentle curves suggest femininity and grace, while bold, strong upright lines look masculine or give a feeling of aspiration. Spirals and curves will seem to dance and suggest movement and rhythm, while low horizontal lines create a mood of stability and peace.

SPACE
When planning a flower arrangement consider the setting or the space in which it will stand. The arrangement needs space around it in order to give it status; if it is crowded with ornaments, photographs and lamps the whole effect of a lovely design will be lost. Try to arrange your flowers in the position in which they will remain so you can gauge the amount of space required around them. Ornaments can be moved or grouped together to accommodate the

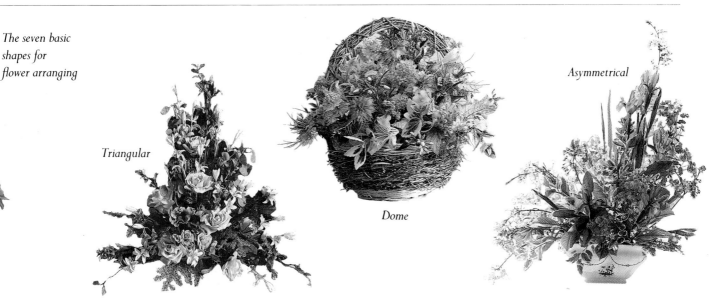

The seven basic shapes for flower arranging

Triangular

Dome

Asymmetrical

arrangement or give it prominence. The correct size of an arrangement to fill a given space is important; try to imagine a cube or rectangle in the space that the completed arrangement will fill.

Space between plant material

Designs which also have interesting spaces between the plant material give an impression of vitality, as the eye can move around freely to observe the relationship of space and solid and can appreciate the qualities of individual plant material.

In order to give an arrangement a lighter effect you can raise it above the level of the table or shelf on which it stands, thereby leaving space beneath the design. Pedestal-type containers, those with feet or a stem and candlesticks with a candle cup are particularly useful here.

When using a heavy, flat container, you will find that long-stemmed plant material will both lift the design, give some space low down and balance the base.

COLOUR

The importance of colour in any art cannot be stressed too much, and the skilful artist learns to understand colour and to use it deliberately to compose a harmonious picture of softly blended hues or to create a dramatic effect with contrasting colours. Always choose colours of flowers and foliage carefully, see how they look side by side, and make sure that they are creating the combined effect you want to achieve.

Reactions to colour are immediate and instinctive. You will vividly recall colours in phrases like 'the girl in the red dress', 'the house with the yellow front door' and 'the room with the blue curtains'. Colour affects mood or feeling, such as a dingy grey, a cheerful yellow or a boring brown; it has apparent temperature – for instance, a warm red or cool green. Colours have symbolic value. Purple and 'royal' blue are associated with royalty, green is sometimes thought to be unlucky and yellow is a cheerful spring colour.

Many occasions have their own special colours, such as ruby or golden weddings, blue for the birth of a boy or pink for a girl, or red for Saint Valentine's Day, and flower colours in arrangements often match the occasion. Just as the artist learns to combine colours to produce the exact tint, tone or shade required to paint a picture, so too must the flower arranger learn to mix and match the colours of the plant material provided by nature and to link them with the container, accessories and setting to create a harmonious effect.

Nature's range of colours is unparalleled, and learning to use her palette to create a pleasing mix of colours is one of the great excitements of flower arranging. It is fun but also quite a challenge to be adventurous with colour. For instance, an eye-catching bowl of many shades of pink ranging from pale baby pink to deep magenta shows bold use of a single colour and will doubtless draw a comment from your friends, while an arrangement of lime green, cream and white can make you feel cooler on a hot summer's day.

Description of colours

A basic understanding of the theory of colour will help you select a harmonious colour scheme and create a balanced effect by careful juxtaposition of colours. Colours differ from one another in hue, value and intensity or chroma.

- *Hue:* pure hues are seen in the spectrum of a rainbow – red, orange, yellow, green, blue and violet; they are the pure unmodified colours.
- *Value:* this refers to the lightness or darkness of a colour, or the tint, tone or shade of a hue.
- *Intensity or chroma:* this means the strength or weakness of a colour – the amount of pure hue present in a particular colour.
- *Neutral colours:* black, white and grey. It is worth noting that white reflects other colours, so that a white flower placed next to a red one will tend to look slightly pink. Black absorbs other colours and can look very dominant unless used with discretion.
- *Neutralized colours:* include beige and other low-intensity colours. These are useful for bases, containers and backgrounds because they enhance other colours. Plant material such as driftwood or fungus are in various neutralized shades.
- *Luminosity:* relates to how visible a colour is in a poor light. Yellow, for instance, is a colour with high luminosity and will show up well in a dark

corner. Blue has a very low luminosity and hardly shows up at all in dull conditions or when seen from a distance. Consequently, those blue irises which looked so striking while you were arranging them on the altar will not show up at all from the back of the church.

● *Advancing and receding colours:* red and orange are very bright and advancing colours; they appear to come towards the viewer, and consequently show up well in an arrangement. Advancing colours are ideal in bold, modern designs; care should be taken with them in a traditional arrangement, however, as they can be very dominant.

Blue and violet are receding colours and appear to move away from the viewer. The careful use of advancing and receding colours helps to give depth to an arrangement of flowers.

Green used on its own is usually regarded as a neutral colour; it neither advances nor recedes. Used together with another colour, however, a different effect is created, for instance red plus green may advance and blue plus green may recede.

● *Warm and cool colours:* the colours of a glowing fire, orange and red, are warm colours, whereas the blue of the sky and the green of leaves give the impression of coolness. The remaining two hues, violet and yellow, appear either warm or cool according to their surroundings.

● *Visual weight and colour:* some colours appear to be visually heavier than others and so can affect the balance of a flower arrangement.

Colours of a dark tonal value appear to be visually heavier in weight than those of a lighter tonal value. Black is the heaviest-looking of all shades and white the lightest. Pure violet is the heaviest and pure yellow is the lightest of the intense colours or hues.

In a flower arrangement colours of equal visual weight do not usually enhance one another and can look rather bland together. Equally, a large amount of visually heavy-looking material in any position in a flower arrangement can upset the visual balance: for instance, if too many heavy-looking colours are placed at the top, an arrangement may look top heavy.

Colours in their surroundings

It is impossible to isolate colours as they are always affected by their surroundings, lighting and nearby colours.

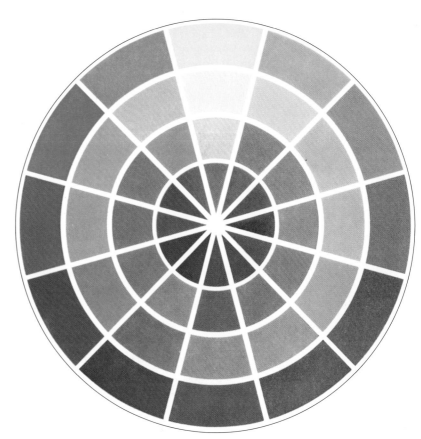

Red and other strong colours alter the adjoining colours with their complementary tones (the opposite colours in the colour wheel): for instance, a red flower could give a greenish tinge to an adjoining white flower, while white and light-coloured flowers also reflect the deeper colours of adjoining flowers or nearby objects.

BASIC COLOUR SCHEMES

Monochromatic schemes
These consist of tints, tones and shades of one colour only. They can produce dull arrangements unless you use diverse shades such as pale pink, dark crimson and a little bright red. You can further enhance such an arrangement with imaginative use of textural contrasts (*see* page 29).

Adjacent schemes
Here two to four colours lying next to each other on the colour wheel are used. An example might be a combination of lime green leaves, and tints, tones and shades of yellow, yellow/orange and orange flowers, in all making a cheerful arrangement for a dull day.

The colour wheel above shows pure hues, tints, tones and shades. In the outer band are the pure hues. The second band shows tints – colours with white added. The third band are tones – hues with grey added – and the inner band are shades, with black added. A monochromatic colour scheme is based on one colour. Adjacent colours can clearly be seen on the colour wheel and complementary colours are those opposite each other, such as violet and yellow. Triadic schemes use three colours equally apart from each other.

A GOOD SELECTION

Triadic colour schemes *of blue/ violet, red/orange and yellow/green flowers and foliage have been successfully created in the arrangement on page 36.*

Polychromatic schemes *of many colours are illustrated on pages 7 and 71 (painting).*

Complementary schemes

Colours opposite each other on the wheel can produce a very satisfactory scheme, but remember that equal amounts of complementary colours can be rather overpowering and you may prefer to use unequal amounts for a more pleasing effect.

Triadic schemes

These schemes use three colours which are equidistant on the colour wheel. The use of the primary hues – red, yellow and blue – could be hard on the eye, whereas tints, tones and shades of these colours would make a more subtle arrangement.

Polychromatic schemes

These use a combination of many colours – Dutch flower paintings are excellent examples of this type of scheme. A harmonious effect can be created using a minimum of strong colour with a large number of tints.

Selecting a colour scheme

1 different combinations of colours can help to create varied moods, atmosphere or effect. Green and white give a feeling of coolness and tranquillity, soft pinks are delicate and pretty, reds and orange are stimulating and shades of yellow have an uplifting effect. Try looking at the colours that surround you, in your home, the garden, the countryside and in shop windows, and see how you react to different colours.

2 use pure hues with restraint as large areas of these colours can be jarring and tiring on the eye. Do not scatter bright colours throughout an arrangement; group them or run a staggered line through the design.

3 repetition of a colour helps to create a harmonious design; for instance, a single brilliant red flower amongst other flowers of different colours attracts the eye far too strongly. Add a few more red flowers and the eye then moves around the design.

4 white flowers too can stand out as bright spots in an arrangement of mixed colours; adding other pale colours will lessen their dominance.

5 schemes using only two colours such as plain green holly (*Ilex* spp.) together with red carnations (*Dianthus* spp.) tend to be lifeless; try adding variegated holly or ivy (*Hedera* spp.) and the arrangement will spring to life. Tints, tones and shades of two colours can make an exciting design.

6 bright colours show up well against dull or neutral backgrounds and containers, whereas colours which recede, such as blue, will seem to disappear in a poor light or when seen from a distance.

7 containers in neutral or neutralized colours or soft greens tone with most shades of flowers and foliage. Other coloured containers should tone with flowers of the same shade in the arrangement so that a harmonious effect is created. White containers can be very eye-catching; they look most attractive when used with white or pale-coloured flowers.

8 with accessories there should be a colour link between the plant material and the accessory. It is not necessary to include all the colours of the accessory in the plant material; just one or two should give the link required to create a harmonious design.

TRICKS WITH COLOUR

Knowing the effects that certain colours or shades produce will help you create atmosphere with an arrangement, give dominance or emphasis to certain areas of it, or achieve a satisfying interplay of contrasting hues.

To increase the apparent size of an object or plant material, use warm hues or colours of full intensity. These colours will also appear to bring an object forward, as will light tints and contrasting colours. They are useful in arrangements which will be seen from a distance. You can also emphasize or create a centre point of an arrangement using warm or strongly contrasting colours. Cool colours, like blue, and dark shades will seem to recede visually.

Complement the mood of a room or create atmosphere with a flower arrangement of cool, light or low intensity hues for a restful ambiance; use warm shades which are less stimulating, for cosiness and colours of full intensity (and some warm shades) for a cheerful environment.

TEXTURE

Generally, flower arrangers work with visual texture, and this type of skilful blending is just as important as the choice and mixing of colours to give visual and tactile satisfaction. Think of the opulence of a smooth satin cushion or the petal of a rose, the richness of velvet curtains or a pansy flower and the warm sheen of a polished wood surface.

TEXTURAL EFFECTS

Depth can be created in a design with the use of texture; for example, a shiny advancing texture can be placed next to a dull receding texture to increase the sense of depth. Your eyes may deceive you when evaluating some textures; a single object or a single flower petal can give an entirely different textural impression from that given by several petals grouped together or that of the whole flower. Just imagine a single pebble on the sea shore; this is smooth and shiny, whereas a bank of pebbles gives the impression of roughness; a single cactus dahlia petal is smooth and satin-like, but the whole flower head is visually spiky.

Lighting has a marked effect on the texture of different surfaces. Try lighting an arrangement from various angles and notice how the contours, shades and amount of reflected light change with each altered position of the lamp. Texture can also be used to create a mood or suggest ideas or feelings; for instance, a bold, rough surface may suggest masculinity and a dull, matt surface can give an aura of sadness.

In minimal arrangements textural interest is a particularly important part of the design; where only essential material and few colours are used, each component is seen clearly, and textural contrasts are needed to give the design impact.

Contrasting textures can enhance one another, whereas two similar textures tend to blend together, giving a blurred effect. For example, a shiny copper or brass container complements rough-textured plant material such as pine cones or a combination of dried yarrow (*Achillea* spp.) and grasses, preserved beech (*Fagus* spp.) (which has a slight sheen) and shiny glycerined laurel (*Laurus* spp.) and mahonia, or Oregon grape, (*Mahonia* spp.) leaves. Satin-like roses (*Rosa* spp.) look wonderful in a matt container, while spikier carnations (*Dianthus* spp.) used with some shiny leaves can look attractive in a container with a high gloss.

Consider as well the surface texture of containers when planning your arrangement. Containers with a light-coloured reflecting surface such as silver, brass, copper, glass and fine porcelain are the most difficult to use as their shiny exterior is very dominant and tends to attract the eye. If you include some plant material with a sheen, this will help reduce the dominance of the container. Whatever the textural quality of the container, including plant material in a similar texture will contribute to the overall harmony of the design.

Colour too is very much affected by texture; on a smooth flat surface some colours appear dull, while on a surface with an interesting texture the same colour can have a much more lively effect. Additionally, rough-textured plant material, particularly flowers, appear darker than flowers with smooth petals.

When using shades of one colour in arrangements a contrast of textures is essential to avoid dullness. This is particularly important in foliage arrangements or when using preserved plant material. In rooms decorated mainly with one colour a variety of textures both in the furnishings and the flower arrangements can transform a potentially dull room into one which is much more exciting.

SELECTING PLANT MATERIAL

When choosing material for a flower arrangement look for enough differences in texture to give a visually balanced effect, but not so many that the design becomes confused. The combinations are endless; the satin-like petals of tulips (*Tulipa* hybrids) may be enhanced by similarly silky pussy willow (*Salix caprea*), matt-textured leaves, soft moss and the roughness of fungi; spiky matt carnations are complemented by smooth, dark green shiny camellia (*Camellia* spp.) leaves or irises (*Iris* spp.). Do not forget the container and accessories. The latter plant combination would look effective in a rough pottery bowl with mottled green Italian arum (*Arum italicum*) leaves at the base, polished pebbles shining through the water and a twisted ivy stem to echo the texture of the container.

Texture is also linked to shape (the shape of carnation petals is what gives them when grouped an apparently spiky texture) as are all the elements of design interlinked, so it is important to visualize the whole arrangement while selecting textures, as well as to imagine the arrangement in its setting.

CREATING TEXTURE IN ARRANGEMENTS

Left: in a monochromatic arrangement plant material of contrasting textures is needed to make the individual flowers stand out. A little foliage will also provide some contrast.

Right: the fluffy mimosa contrasts well with the soft, broad-leaved tulips, smooth green leaves and glass vase.

Left: the dramatic shadows cast by the candlelight emphasize the texture of the red gerbera petals and show up the yellow centres of the flowers.

Right: this modern design shows stark contrasts of texture between the smooth, shiny black container, the ridged red flowers and the fatsia leaf reflecting the light. The twigs and container link.

Left: the spiky twig basket, rosemary leaves and love-in-a-mist flowers are complemented by the smoother material.

Right: note the textural and colour links between the candle, chair backs, glasses and plant material. The plant material picks out the brown and beige colours of the harvest fare to highlight the festive theme.

THE PRINCIPLES OF DESIGN

The Principles of Design are the basic laws governing any art form. All great works of art have aesthetically pleasing proportions, rhythm, movement, areas of contrast and emphasis and, above all, a harmonious appearance. The latter is derived from all of these elements, which together make up a well-balanced whole. The same general principles can be applied to flower arranging, taking into account the nature of the material you are using and the specific kind of effect or atmosphere you are trying to achieve.

SCALE

The scale of any design refers to the size relationship of all its individual parts and to the design as a whole within its setting. In a flower arrangement there are many parts of the design which need to be related in size to ensure that they are in proportion. These include the setting, the plant material, container, any accessories used and the base on which the flower arrangement may stand.

The setting

The size of both the flower arrangement and the plant material used must relate to the size of the setting. While a petite arrangement with small, delicate flowers would look lost on a heavy oak chest in a hall it would appear just right on a bedside table. Equally, large flower arrangements which can be seen at a distance would be in the correct scale for a cathedral setting.

Plant material

To achieve a good design the scale relationship between each flower and the foliage used must be correct. For example, a violet (*Viola* spp.) and a paeony (*Paeonia* spp.) would not blend happily together, and so some gradation in size between both smaller and larger material is necessary for a more harmonious effect.

The scale of this simple arrangement of small, delicate flowers in a glass bowl is particularly suitable for a dressing-table. Fill up small containers with water daily to prevent drying out. The fine-stemmed flowers are supported by the bushy heathers.

Flowers & foliage:

MAUVE AND PINK HEATHER, PALE YELLOW PRIMROSES, BLUE GRAPE HYACINTHS, BLUE SIBERIAN SQUILL, IVY LEAVES.

The container

This too has to be considered in relation to the size of the plant material used in it and also to the scale of the whole design. Accordingly, a hydrangea (*Hydrangea* spp.) in a wine glass or primroses (*Primula* spp.) in a large bowl would look wrong.

Accessories

These must relate to size and scale. For instance, a dainty figurine will require smaller flowers than those used to complement a sculpted bust of the same height. Additionally the size of the *whole* arrangement should be in scale with the accessory. If an accessory looks too small in relation to the arrangement, place it towards the front of the design or raise it to make it look larger than it really is. A group of two or three small accessories, perhaps at different levels, can give the illusion of a larger whole. An accessory that is too large can seem smaller if you place it towards the back of the design.

Bases

These too should be in scale with the whole design. If you use a small container or a well pinholder on a covered base or a slice of wood, the plant material must be in scale with the base rather than the container. The diameter of the base, and not the size of the small container, limits the size of the design.

Arrangements

Scale is especially important in the following arrangements:

● *Miniature or very tiny arrangements:* it is particularly important that all the components are in scale both with each other and with the completed design. The plant material must be naturally small, rather than cut down from larger material; the container too should be tiny, and if a base is used it should also be small, neither too thick nor heavy-looking, or it would dominate the design.

● *Large pedestal arrangements:* in this type of arrangement the whole design might stand 4 feet (120 cm) tall. Use large, bold and dramatic plant material. False castor-oil plant (*Fatsia japonica*), large bergenia (*Bergenia* spp.) and plantain lily (*Hosta* spp.) leaves are suitable, as are large dahlias (*Dahlia* hybrids), hydrangeas (*Hydrangea* spp.), lilies (*Lilium* spp.) and paeonies (*Paeonia* spp.), delphiniums (*Delphinium* spp.) or bells of Ireland (*Molucella laevis*).

PROPORTION

Proportion, the correct relation of one thing to another or between parts of a thing, relates to measurements or quantities in comparison with each other.

The proportions of an arrangement in a stemmed container are based on the Golden Section. The plant material should be about one and a half times the height of the container, in other words in the proportion of three to two. In addition, when using a low, wide bowl or a low container on a base, the height of the plant material should be one and a half times the width of the bowl or base to give the most pleasing proportion.

It is not always easy to differentiate between scale and proportion: scale is concerned with relative sizes, while proportion concentrates on relative amounts. For example, the leaves and flowers may be in scale with the size of a container; if, however, there is too much plant material in the container then the arrangement will not have pleasing proportions. In addition, if a small room is overfilled with nicely scaled arrangements the effect will be wrong because the number of arrangements will not be in proportion to the size of the room.

In a flower arrangement, equal amounts of components may produce an uninteresting design, and so may too much of one component, such as a heavy-looking base, too many large, bright flowers or a lot of very tall plant material in a small container.

Generally, it is not possible to work to exact measurements in flower arranging; the eye is the best judge of pleasing and correct proportion.

BALANCE

The state of stability, equilibrium or equal weight defined by balance is achieved in two ways within flower arranging.

Actual balance refers to an arrangement which is balanced in weight and literally will not fall over. Florist's foam or a pinholder are particularly useful for stability.

When arranging flowers on a windowsill or on a narrow shelf, well-fixed mechanics and a heavy container or pinholder are essential, as the weight of the plant material at the front of the design might otherwise cause the arrangement to fall forward.

Visual balance is assessed by the eye: ask yourself whether the arrangement looks unstable, does it have the appearance of being top- or bottom-heavy or lopsided, does it lean forwards or backwards? These factors must be corrected for the arrangement to look visually balanced.

Luminous, very dark or bright colours can make an arrangement seem unbalanced if they are dominant. So too can large or round flower shapes, shiny or very rough textures and dense, compact-looking forms. Do not place an arrangement in a small, enclosed space, or it will over-dominate the area.

Symmetrical and asymmetrical designs

The outline of a symmetrically balanced arrangement is the same on either side of an imaginary horizontal or vertical central line. The plant material need not be exactly the same on either side of the central line: it may vary in size, texture, number and variety; nevertheless the arrangement should still look visually balanced within the design.

Asymmetrical designs can be visually more stimulating than symmetrical ones – they are sometimes called dynamic designs – and consist of dissimilar material of equal dominance placed on either side of an imaginary vertical or horizontal central line. For example, two or three large bergenia leaves placed low down and to one side of the imaginary line will balance much longer and finer leaves low down on the opposite side of the line.

Balance within the setting

Some arrangements may look unbalanced because they are not placed in the correct position on the table, base or shelf on which they are to stand. This applies in particular to asymmetrical designs in which longer plant material protrudes on one side to balance shorter, heavier-looking material on the other side. If you place the container off-centre with the heavier material near to the edge of the table, base or shelf, you will obtain a more satisfactory sense of balance. Additionally, if you decide not to focus the centre of interest of an arrangement over the centre of a container, the design will look balanced when centred in the middle of the table or base.

Accessories

As indicated earlier, you should place an accessory in position *before* the plant material is arranged. If you do this after the arrangement is completed, its visual weight may upset the balance of the design. Moreover, the visual weight of a large accessory may be reduced by placing it close to the flower arrangement.

RHYTHM

In any art form rhythm is used to give life and interest to a design through repetition, sequence, areas of movement and areas of rest, all of which contribute to a harmonious whole.

Good use of rhythm makes a flower arrangement much more interesting; the eye is able to move easily through the design with various rests, pauses and motion. The rapidity with which the eye moves through the design depends on the type of material used. A straight line accelerates the movement, an undulating curve gives a slow, gentle rhythm and a brightly coloured round flower arrests the eye and creates a pause in the movement. It also evokes an atmosphere or mood; for instance, bold curves will give a strong sense of rhythm and convey a dancing movement.

There are three principal ways in which rhythm can be created in a flower arrangement: by the use of repetition, transition and radiation.

● *Repetition:* helps to give movement to an arrangement. Forms, lines, colours and textures need to be repeated so that they form a path which takes the eye over the design. A single flower of a dominant shape or colour will always catch your attention, but if you repeat the same shape or colour the eye will follow in a line to the part of the design where it is repeated.

● *Transition:* implies a gradual change from one colour to another, one size to another and one form to another. If you look at a tree in winter-time, your eye flows easily along the broad trunk out to the wider branches and slender twigs, following a gradual change in size. Equally, a gladiolus spike shows a gradual change in form and size from wide open flowers at the base to closed buds at the tip of the stem.

In traditional arrangements transitional movement lends gentle rhythm as size and colour change from the larger, darker flowers in the centre to the smaller flowers at the extremities. In modern and more simple designs you can create a strong and exciting rhythm by making less use of transition and greater use of contrast.

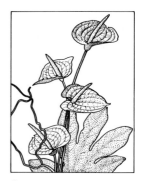

Repetition

Transition

Radiation

Removing surplus twigs and leaves to give a clean line to an arrangement.

CONTRASTING FLOWER SHAPES

Rounds or points
Rose, dahlia, paeony, geranium, tulip.

Lines
Lavender, buddleia, delphinium, reedmace or bulrushes (cattails).

Transitional
Columbine, honeysuckle, gypsophila, mimosa, sweet pea.

● *Radiation:* a different type of rhythm gives to a design by the use of radiating lines. Nature provides many examples: the branches of a bare winter tree radiate out from the trunk, the veins of a geranium (*Pelargonium* spp.) leaf radiate from the point at which they join the stem and the petals of a daisy radiate from the centre of the flower.

The rhythm of radiation is used mainly in traditional designs, where the plant material radiates from the rim of the container.

Movement and the whole design
When planning a flower arrangement consider the rhythm of the whole design. This includes the plant material, container, base and any accessories used. For example, a figurine portraying a ballet dancer could be complemented by swirling willow bent to echo the shape of the figurine, or the curve of a jug handle could be copied in the shape of plant material used within the jug.

Rhythm and plant material
Arrange the plant material with the movement and atmosphere of the design in mind. An unco-ordinated mass of material with crossing stems and overlapping or superfluous leaves and flowers has no rhythm, whereas the removal of excess twigs from a branch, fussy buds from a flower spray and surplus leaves from foliage helps to give a clean line and definite movement to the arrangement.

CONTRAST AND VARIETY
Designs without variation or contrast do not hold your attention because they lack vitality; even a slight variation will increase your interest considerably.

In traditional designs variations on a theme are used rather than strong contrasts of colour, shape, texture or size. In modern designs, where a minimal amount of plant material is used, strong contrasts which need more space around them create a dramatic effect and emphasize the individual components of the design.

Creating contrast
● *Colour:* bold, striking effects with colour can be created with opposite colours on the colour wheel, such as blue and orange, red and green or yellow and purple. Strong contrasts can also be created with red and black. Subtle colour schemes use various tints, tones and shades of one colour or adjacent colours on the colour wheel – *see* page 27.

● *Shape:* a design consisting entirely of rounds or of pointed shapes could be very dull. Remember that rounds can be turned and used in profile for a different shape and contrasting shapes can enhance the beauty of the individual forms. Contrasting shapes can be adventurously used, such as sword-like iris leaves and large, round bergenia leaves.

● *Texture:* contrasting textures can also give excitement and life to a design. You might place a smooth lily petal against rough driftwood, a smooth, shining camellia leaf with a spiky cactus dahlia or fluffy mimosa, or silver wattle, (*Acacia dealbata*) and satiny tulips in a matt container.

Dried flower arrangements need strong textural contrasts in order to give the design life and to avoid a monotonous appearance.

The whole design
Contrast and variety should form part of the whole design in its setting. Your aim should be to create an arrangement which contrasts harmoniously with its background. It should neither blend so closely with it that it disappears nor should strong colours clash. Consider how fitting bases, containers and figurines are for the arrangement and setting.

However diverse your materials, all the elements of design – colour, shape, texture and lines of movement – must balance and relate to create a unified whole.

DOMINANCE OR EMPHASIS
Just as an actor takes a leading part in a play and is supported by actors in lesser roles, so there are parts in any design which are more dominant than others, and their interplay makes for a unified whole.

In a flower arrangement the plant material normally predominates over other components of the design. Some areas should also predominate over others within the arrangement of flowers and leaves, leading the eye through the design.

When your flower arrangement is completed, look at the *whole* design and if some part should appear too dominant, try to remedy the situation. You could move a dominant figurine nearer to the arrangement, replace a heavy-looking base with a thinner one in a lighter colour or change a dominant shiny or white container for one of a darker colour and matt texture. Within the arrangement itself, turning around flowers to reduce their dominance, reducing the amount of shiny material and introducing tints and tones of a strong colour will all help draw the eye away from the dominant colour.

Remember that you want your best and most beautiful plant material in dominant positions, but it must be backed up by the other plant material for a unified design.

LIGHTING

Just as there is no colour without light, so light is needed also to make forms visible. Good lighting is particularly important to a flower arranger, as it is to an artist who works in three dimensions. It will help give depth to a design, with the contrast of light and shadow strengthening the various forms within the design.

The effect of lighting on colour
Colour is not only dependent on light for its existence, but its effect and appearance are altered by the type and quality of light on it. Lighting in a room varies depending upon the time of day, the season and the type of artificial lighting used. Four walls may have been painted with the same pot of paint, but the colour may appear quite different on each wall, according to how much and what kind of light is available in areas of the same room.

Different types of lighting
Natural light or daylight varies considerably according to the time of day, season or weather conditions. Strong daylight enhances most colours, particularly blue.

Tungsten electric lighting gives a yellowish light in which blues and mauves recede. This light does, however, enhance reds, oranges, yellows and cream.

White fluorescent lighting gives a very flat shadowless light that causes reds to appear brownish and dull. Blues and violets are brightened by this light.

Candlelight is soft, but reds, dark colours and shades of blue and mauve can appear very dull in it. Luminous colours such as yellow, orange, pale pink or white show up well.

Lighting and texture
Lighting greatly affects the appearance of texture. Do not light arrangements face on or this will appear to flatten any texture. Strong lighting makes very shiny or rough textures eye-catching and they advance visually, whereas smooth, dull or blurred textures appear to recede. The shadows caused by a half light emphasize the texture of a rough surface.

HARMONY

Proper use of the principles and elements of design give harmony and unity to an arrangement. Before composing the design, consider the setting: there should be harmony of colour, style, size and character between the arrangement and the room in which it is to stand. Do not clutter the space which the completed arrangement is to occupy with the other objects in the room and allow the space to be large enough for the arrangement to be seen to advantage and to be a harmonious addition to the room's décor.

Flowers and foliage within a design should harmonize with each other naturally, as should the type of material and container. For instance, sophisticated material and fussy wild flowers do not harmonize well, nor do lovely longiflorum lilies in a rustic container.

The spacing of the plant material in the container is an important aspect of an arrangement. If the flowers and foliage are too crowded or overlapping, the harmony is lost. The visual balance of the arrangement needs to be pleasing to the eye, and the plant material should appear to sit happily in the container.

The size difference of the plant material should not be too great, the flowers and foliage need to be in scale with the container, while the whole arrangement needs to be in scale with its setting. The amount of plant material within the container, its form and shape and the amount of dominant material are also relevant. In addition, there should not be too many arrangements for the size of the room.

The repetition of colour, forms, shapes, lines and texture also has a unifying effect and is one of the simplest ways to achieve rhythmic harmony both within the arrangement of flowers and between other components of the design.

The texture and colour of the plant material, the setting, container, accessories and the base or surface on which the arrangement is to stand should all harmonize with each other. Harsh contrasts, too much variety in plant material, and

---

FLOWERS FOR SOPHISTICATED AND RUSTIC CONTAINERS

Sophisticated
Lilies, carnations, orchids

Rustic
Ox-eye daisies, cow parsley, monkshood, chrysanthemums and many wild flowers.

Far left: daylight from a window enhances the natural colours of flowers. Small orange flowers are used with discretion, while pale foliage provides a loose framework for this delicate design.

Flowers & foliage:

ORANGE MONTBRETIA, ORANGE SAFFLOWER (FALSE SAFFRON), BLUE SCABIOUS, BLUE BELLFLOWER, DARK BLUE LARKSPUR, PALE BLUE LOVE-IN-A-MIST FLOWERS AND GREEN SEED HEADS, CREAM SWEET PEAS, VARIEGATED ACER *NEGUNDO ELEGANTISSIMUM*.

Left: a lamp is used to suffuse these blue delphiniums with yellow light and give tonal variation to the arrangement. This in turn emphasizes texture.

Flowers & foliage:

BLUE DELPHINIUMS, CREAM JAPANESE ANEMONE LEAVES.

Mechanics: CHICKEN WIRE.

the over-dominance of some flowers, foliage or the base or container can produce a jarring note.

Consider the various forms of lighting, too. The colour and texture of the material used in arrangements needs to be viewed both in the various forms of artificial lighting as well as in daylight to ensure that the arrangement harmonizes with the rest of the room and that it shows to best advantage.

Finally, observation will increase your knowledge of harmony: the shades of colour in a single flower, the complementary shapes of the flowers and foliage on a growing plant, the branches and leaves of a tree, the colours of a sunset, a piece of material or an attractively dressed shop window. Look around and observe and some combinations of colours or shapes may well inspire you to create a really exciting design.

SHAPE AND STYLE

*E*VERY ROOM HAS A CERTAIN STYLE in its architecture and in the furniture, soft furnishings and *objets d'art* within it. Flower arrangements need to harmonize with the décor: a mass arrangement would suit a Victorian drawing-room and a simple or free-form design would complement a modern apartment.

TRADITIONAL OR MASS

Popular for a long time, these designs have developed from a rather solid-looking arrangement with little space between the flowers to a much looser and more flowing style which allows the butterflies to fly through.

The outline of the arrangement conforms to a geometric shape with seven basic outlines: horizontal, vertical, symmetrical and asymmetrical triangles, dome-shaped, crescent-shaped and S-shaped (Hogarth curve). Each one incorporates a similar basic design: the stems radiate out from a point in the centre – the area of interest – with transition in size and colour. The larger, more dominant material is in the centre and the finer, lighter material at the extremities of the design. The colours are very harmonious with little contrast in colour, form or size. The plant material consists of many varieties, often of horticultural interest; depth is created in areas where plant material recedes.

CONSTRUCTING A TRADITIONAL (TRIANGULAR) ARRANGEMENT

Many traditional designs are constructed in low bowls or containers with a stem, such as an urn. The following instructions are for an arrangement using florist's foam.

1 secure a foam holder in the base of the container.

2 cut a square block of foam which will fit into the container leaving space for water at the sides; the foam should project about 1½ inches (4 cm) above the rim of the container.

3 soak the foam and place it in the container; a large design will require a cap of 2 inch (5 cm) chicken wire firmly taped into the container.

4 since any arrangement must incorporate

STAGE **4**

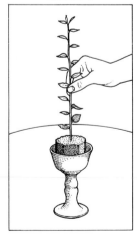

height, width and depth, begin the design with an outline of fine, pointed material. Define the height with a straight stem about one to one and a half times the height of the container. This first stem should be inserted in the foam about two-thirds of the distance from the front (*see* far left).

5 push the stem well into the foam.

STAGE **6**

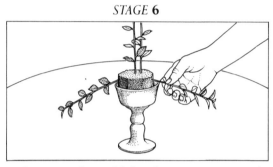

6 determine the width by placing a stem on each side of the block of foam flowing downward slightly; the three points of the triangle are now established. The remaining stems should radiate from the centre outwards, keeping within the imaginary triangle formed by the first three stems (above).

7 create depth by placing some stems to the front and rear of the design.

STAGE **8**

8 the next stage is to create the most eye-catching part of the arrangement (above). Place the most dominant flower at a point just above the base of the main stem with three or five larger leaves radiating out from it to give extra strength to the centre.

9 place staggered lines of plant material radiating out from the centre and decreasing in size towards the outer edges. Remember to place material to the back of the design to create depth and to give an even balance to the arrangement so that it does not fall over.

STAGE **10**

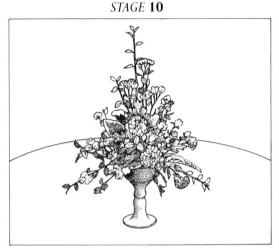

10 fill in with transitional material – material which is half-way in size and colour intensity between outline and central material (above). Note: When you are using a selection of different colours, try to group them in a harmonious manner; for instance, dominant colours such as red or white can give a spotted effect if scattered indiscriminately throughout the design.

11 finally, check your arrangement from all angles, ensuring that the foam or wire is not visible and that there is sufficient space between the flowers to show each one to advantage.

12 carefully fill up the container with water using a long-spouted watering-can, then sit back and enjoy your creation.

SIMPLE, MODERN OR FREE-FORM

Modern designs differ from traditional ones in the restrained use of plant material and the creation of a striking and dramatic design. The emphasis is on bold and interesting plant material shown to great effect by the use of space within the design. The shape is usually free-form without a geometric silhouette, and the plant material is selected for its form, texture and interest, often rising above the rim of the container, which forms an important part of the design. The emphasis is on strong line, and in some designs there may be more than one centre of interest. For instance, cane or vines can be formed into loops, and the 'enclosed' space created will then balance a more solid-looking flower or leaf. Very often the container is an important part of the design.

Simple designs also use few flowers and leaves, but have a less clear form and outline.

CONSTRUCTING A MODERN ARRANGEMENT

Modern arrangements appear very simple to the eye, but their design requires some thought, particularly regarding the dominance and balance of the various components. Here are two ideas:

STAGE **1**

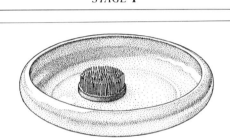

STAGE **2**

1 begin with a wide, shallow bowl into which a pinholder is fixed slightly off centre (above).

2 insert three irises on to the pinholder in gradated steps, each one facing a slightly different direction (right).

STAGE **3**

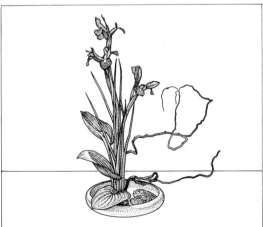

3 insert sparse, twiggy branches flowing out nearly horizontally on one side of the irises. Weight can be provided at the base of the design with two or three large leaves placed to one side and a few stones in the water on the other side.

A double arrangement with just two large flowers makes an economical and attractive design:

1 place a tall cylindrical container and a matching shorter one on a base such as a wood slice. Use pinholders and/or chicken wire in the taller cylinder as mechanics.

2 insert a piece of curved, fine driftwood about one and a half times the height of the taller container, then insert another piece into the lower container to balance the first and curve around the taller container.

3 place one or two large leaves in the lower container on the side farthest away from the taller one, then one large leaf on the other side in the tall cylinder.

4 lastly, place a large flower just above the leaves in both containers. Large chrysanthemums, lilies, dahlias and rhododendrons (*Rhododendron* spp.) are all suitable flowers for this arrangement.

Once you have completed your arrangement of flowers try to assess it objectively. Ask yourself whether the arrangement is appropriate to the occasion and the setting, whether it is interesting and imaginative, whether the selection of material and everything used are suitable and harmonious. Is anything superfluous – does each part of the design contribute to the whole for a unified effect? Does the arrangement give you pleasure, have you achieved something new with a different style or unusual container? Is your design all you hoped it would be?

This formal pink, orange and white arrangement takes its colour scheme from adjacent colours on the colour wheel. Contrasting textures and shapes and dark, clearly defined foliage give the design impact.

Flowers & foliage:

PINK GERBERAS, ORANGE AND PALE PINK CARNATIONS, ORANGE AND DEEP PINK SPRAY CARNATIONS, CHAMPAGNE ROSES, PALE PINK SPRAY SINGLE CHRYSANTHEMUMS, LIME TREE LEAF BUDS, *COTONEASTER FRANCHETII*, YEW, BERGENIA LEAVES, BROWN GLYCERINED BEECH.

Mechanics:

FLORIST'S FOAM, CHICKEN WIRE, TAPE.

A horizontal pastel arrangement which suits its surroundings: the pale colours of the flowers tone with those of the fireplace, painting and frame, neither dominating nor detracting from the principal point of interest, the painting. The shape of the arrangement mirrors the shapes of the leafy designs above and below it of the picture frame and fireplace.

Flowers & foliage:

VERY PALE PINK SPRAY CHRYSANTHEMUMS, WHITE FREESIAS, CHAMPAGNE ROSES, WHITE CHERRY BLOSSOM, COW PARSLEY, GREY-GREEN EUCALYPTUS, RUE, JEW'S MALLOW.

Mechanics: TWO PINHOLDERS, NYLON JERSEY MATERIAL, FLORIST'S FOAM, CHICKEN WIRE, TAPE.

TRADITION AND STYLE

A STYLISH ARRANGEMENT usually makes a statement of some sort which is derived from your individual choice of flowers and the way in which you have chosen to arrange them (whether formally and traditionally or informally). Brightly coloured, round flowers massed in a container will make a bold statement. Delicate transitional flower shapes and trailing foliage will give a gentle image, which is more subtly conveyed.

If you wish to make a statement with your arrangements or evoke a certain mood, it is useful to be aware not only of the impact of certain shapes and colours, but also of the background traditions, mythology or history of certain flowers and plants. Many were once used for medicinal purposes, others were named after gods or have symbolic value – the most well-known example of the latter is the rose, which has long had romantic associations.

Paeony *(Paeonia)*

The native European paeony (Officianalis) is found throughout the continent from France to Albania; other varieties come from India, China and Siberia.

The paeony is said to take its name from the young god Paeon, a pupil of the Greek god of medicine. One day, while wandering near Mount Olympus, he discovered an unusual plant which alleviated the pains of women in childbirth. He subsequently became such a successful physician that he incurred the jealousy of his master and was turned into a plant, the paeony. Paeonies have been cultivated throughout the ages for their beautiful colour and form as well as for medicinal purposes. The bold, round form of these flowers renders them ideal for the centres of large arrangements, and their deep-cut leaves make striking foliage.

Bull Bay *(Magnolia grandiflora)*

This most spectacular flowering tree originated in Bull Bay in the south-eastern United States. The dark green, glossy, ovate leaves have a rust-coloured felt on the undersides. The tree needs the protection of a wall in cooler climes and will grow to a height of 10 to 15 feet (3 to 5 metres). The large, cream-coloured, fragrant flowers appear from July to September.

Doctor Magnol first produced the idea of classifying plants, which was later carried out by Linnaeus. The Magnolia tree was named in Magnol's honour in 1753, for his services to horticulture at Montpellier Botanic Garden.

The glossy, bold shapes of the leaves are useful to the flower arranger to strengthen the centre of large designs. They glycerine well and the leaves can be wired individually for use in preserved arrangements.

Larkspur *(Delphinium consolida)*

This delightful flower, which is found in shades of blue, purple, red, pink and white, is the ancestor of border delphiniums. Larkspur is a hardy annual which flowers in the summer. It provides useful line material for flower arrangements.

Delphinium consolida was said to be a powerful plant for healing wounds — hence the Latin name 'consolida', which means 'to unite'. The name larkspur is derived from the spur-like projections on the flowers. It was also known as lark's heels, toes, and claws, and is associated with the month of July. It would be particularly appropriate in an arrangement for a friend whose birthday falls in that month.

Iris *(Iris cv.)*

The iris is a genus of 300 flowering plants which are found throughout the Northern Hemisphere. The long-lasting, sword-like leaves make useful line material for both traditional and modern flower arrangements.

The flowers come in many shades and are named after Iris, the goddess of the rainbow. She acted as a messenger between the gods and the mortals, bridging the gap between earth and sky.

The flower is commemorated on a carved marble panel in the Temple of Karnak in Egypt. The Egyptians prized it for its medicinal qualities and also used it to make love potions. Orris or iris root was also used in the Middle Ages for medicinal purposes, and for making perfume. The powdered roots are still used today as a perfume fixative for scents and pot-pourri.

Stinking Hellebore *(Helleborus foetidus)*

The clusters of pale green flowers and dark green palmate leaves of the hellebore have a somewhat sinister history. The hellebore is cathartic, but poisonously so. The plants used to be given to children to cure worms, often with fatal results. It is well named, as the word 'Hellebore' derives from the Greek 'helein', meaning 'to kill' and 'bora', meaning 'food'. The Latin 'foetidus' refers to the plant's unpleasant smell.

The green flowers of the hellebore appear early in the year and, despite the plant's dramatic associations, are useful transitional material for arrangements of spring flowers. The dark green leaves are evergreen. Plants will thrive in almost any situation, but once established do not like to be disturbed. The hellebore is a welcome addition to the garden when few other flowers are in bloom.

Rose *(Rosa cv.)*

Roses are ancient plants, described in the third century BC by the philosopher Theophrastus in his Enquiry into Plants. *The rose is the flower of Venus, goddess of love, and has long had romantic associations. It is mentioned 70 times in Shakespeare's plays and sonnets, and the red rose is the most popular flower for Saint Valentine's Day gifts. The rose became symbolic for the early Christians, symbolizing the wounds of Christ and blood of the early martyrs.*

The rose is probably the most loved of garden plants. The leaves make useful transitional material for arrangements, and can be removed from the stem and used separately within the arrangement.

Far left: the simple shapes and colour contrasts of the flowers and foliage lend repetition and variety respectively. The neutral container shows off the bright flowers to best advantage.

Flowers & foliage:

DOUBLE CREAM AND YELLOW DAFFODILS, YELLOW NARCISSUS 'CHEERFULNESS', GREEN AND PURPLE LENTEN ROSE, BRIGHT PINK TULIPS, CERISE SPRAY CARNATIONS, *VIBURNUM GRANDIFLORUM*.

Mechanics:

PINHOLDER, CHICKEN WIRE.

Left: the colour for a golden wedding anniversary is reflected in this pedestal arrangement, which complements the traditional décor.

Flowers & foliage:

YELLOW FORSYTHIA, ROSES, SPRAY CARNATIONS, SPIDER CHRYSANTHEMUMS, CREAM FREESIAS, WHITE SPIRAEA 'BRIDAL WREATH', ROSEMARY FOLIAGE, SKIMMIA JAPONICA LEAVES.

Mechanics: FOAM HOLDER, FLORIST'S FOAM, TAPE.

DIRECTORY OF FLOWERS AND FOLIAGE

THE FOLLOWING DIRECTORY is a guide to the conditioning and preserving methods given for various types of flowers and foliage, which are divided according to the time of year when they grow. Where a conditioning method is not indicated, no treatment is necessary other than cutting the stems on a slant and giving the plant material a drink in deep water; where no preserving method is shown, flowers or foliage can only be used fresh. All the main types of flowers and foliage used in this book are listed, but there are many more to choose from and myriad ways of combining fresh and preserved material in arrangements.

TYPE		CONDITIONING	PRESERVING
B = Bulb **T** = Tree **C** = Climber **Wc** = Woody climber **Cm** = Corm **G** = Greenhouse **Cn** = Cone **Bi** = Biennial **Fr** = Fibrous rooted **Bb** = Bamboo-like **Ha** = Hardy annual ***** = Fragrant **P** = Perennial **sh** = seed heads **R** = Rhizome **l** = leaves **S** = Shrub **d** = double **Sp** = Seedpod **s** = single		Special conditioning and preserving techniques for flowers and foliage are described in detail in Tricks of the Trade. **1** = Boiling water treatment **2** = Seal ends in flame **3** = Plug **4** = Scrape **5** = Slit **6** = Submerge	**A1** = Air drying 1 (hanging) **A2** = Air drying 2 (in water) **A3** = Air drying 3 (in newspaper) **D** = Desiccants **F** = Pressing in flower press specifically **G1** = Glycerine – Method 1 **G2** = Glycerine – Method 2 **P1** = Pressing in flower press or book **P2** = Pressing between sheets of newspaper

FLOWERS

LATIN NAME	COMMON NAME	TYPE	White	Cream	Yellow	Orange	Red	Brown	Purple	Mauve	Pink	Blue	Green	SPECIAL CONDITIONING	PRESERVING
SPRING															
Acacia dealbata	Mimosa (silver wattle)	T			●									5, 1	A1
Alstroemerias	Peruvian lily	P	●		●	●	●		●		●			–	D
Anemone coronaria	Windflower	Cm	●				●		●	●	●	●		–	D2, P1
Aquilegia	Columbine	P	●	●	●	●	●		●	●	●	●	●	–	P1
Brodiaea	Brodiaeas	C							●	●	●	●		–	P1
Calluna vulgaris	Heather or ling	S								●				–	A2
Campanula glomerata	Clustered wallflower	P	●						●					–	P1
Ceanothus	Californian lilac	S										●		5	–
Chamelaucium uncinatum	Geraldtom wax plant (Wax flower)	S	●				●		●		●			5	–
Cheiranthus cheiri*	Common or English wallflower	P			●		●			●	●			1	P1

46

LATIN NAME	COMMON NAME	TYPE	White	Cream	Yellow	Orange	Red	Brown	Purple	Mauve	Pink	Blue	Green	SPECIAL CONDITIONING	PRESERVING
*Choisya ternata**	Mexican orange	S	●											5, 1	–
Convallaria majalis	Lily of the valley	R	●							●				–	D
*Endymion**	Wild hyacinths or English bluebells (Wood hyacinth)	B	●							●	●			–	D
Erysimum alpinus	Alpine wallflower	P			●	●			●					1	P
Forsythia	Forsythia	S			●									5	F, D
Galanthus	Snowdrops	B	●											–	P1
Helleborus foetidus	Stinking hellebore	P											●	1	D, G1
Helleborus orientalis	Lenten rose	P	●	●			●	●	●		●			1	D, G1
*Hyacinthus**	Hyacinth	B	●		●	●				●	●			–	D
Impatiens bolstii	Busy Lizzie	P	●			●				●	●			–	P1
Intermedia suspensa	Weeping forsythia	S			●									1	P1
Iris	Iris	R	●		●				●			●		–	–
Jasminium nudiflorium	Winter jasmine	S			●									5	–
Kolkwitzia anabilis	Beauty bush	S									●			5	–
Laburnum anagyroides	Golden laburnum (Golden chain)	T			●									5, 1	–
Lamium	Dead nettle	P	●	●	●									–	P1
Leptospermum scoparium	Tea tree – New Zealand	S	●							●	●			5	–
Leucanthemum vulgare	Ox-eye daisy	P	●		●									–	P1
*Lonicera periclymenum**	Climbing honeysuckle (Woodbine)	Wc	●	●	●				●		●			5	–
Lonicera tatarica	Tartarian honeysuckle	S	●								●			5	–
Lunaria annua	Honesty (Silver dollar)	Ha	●										●	–	A1
Muscari	Grape hyacinth	B	●		●							●	●	–	–
Myosotis sylvatica	Forget-me-not	Ha	●								●	●		–	P1
*Narcissus**	Daffodils	B	●	●	●									–	P1, D
Nepeta faassenii	Catmint	P							●	●		●		–	A1
Pelargonium zonale	Geranium	S	●	●	●	●	●		●	●	●			–	P1
*Polyanthus primula**	Primroses	P	●	●	●	●	●		●	●	●	●		–	P1, D
Prunus conradinae	Ornamental cherry	T	●								●			5, 4, 1	P1
*Prunus yedoensis**	Yoshimo cherry (Japanese flowering cherry)	T	●								●			5, 1	P1
Ribes sanguineum	Flowering currant	S					●				●			5	–
*Rosmarinus officinalis**	Rosemary	S	●						●			●		5	A1
Scilla siberica	Siberian squill	B	●						●			●		–	P1
Spiraea	Spiraea	S	●				●				●			5, 1	–
*Syringa vulgaris**	Common lilac	S, T	●						●	●				5, 1	–
Tulipa	Tulip	B	●	●	●	●	●	●	●	●	●	●	●	–	P1
Viburnum tinus	Laurustinus	S	●								●			5, 1	–
Viola wittrockiana	Garden pansy	Ha	●	●	●	●		●	●	●		●		–	P1
Weigela	Weigela	S	●				●		●		●			5, 4	–
*Zantedeschia**	Arum lily (Calla lily)	R	●										●	–	–
SUMMER															
Achillea	Yarrow	P	●		●						●			–	A1, A2
Aconitum	Monkshood	P	●		●							●		1	–
Alchemilla mollis	Lady's mantle	P											●	–	P1, G1
Allium giganteum	Ornamental onions	B							●					–	A1
Amaranthus caudatus	Love-lies-bleeding	Ha					●							1	A1
Anapthalis	Pearly everlasting	P	●											–	A1

LATIN NAME	COMMON NAME	TYPE	White	Cream	Yellow	Orange	Red	Brown	Purple	Mauve	Pink	Blue	Green	SPECIAL CONDITIONING	PRESERVING
Anemone hupehensis	Japanese anemone	Fr	●						●					–	P1
Anthriscus sylvestris	Cow parsley	Ha	●											1	P1
Anthurium andreanum	Painter's palette (Flamingo lily)	G		●			●				●			–	–
Antirrhinum	Snapdragon	Ha	●	●	●	●	●	●	●	●	●		●	1	–
Aquilegia	Columbine	P	●	●	●	●	●	●	●	●	●	●	●	–	P1
Astrantia major	Masterwort	P	●						●	●	●			–	–
Bouvardia	Sweet bouvardia	S	●		●		●				●			1	–
Campanula glomerata	Clustered bellflower	P	●						●			●		–	F
Campanula persicifolia	Peach-leaved or willow bellflower	P	●						●			●		–	F
Carthamus tinctorius	Safflower (False saffron)	Ha			●	●	●							–	A1
Ceanothus	Californian lilac (Redroot)	S	●									●		5	–
Centaurea cyanus	Cornflower	Ha	●				●		●		●	●		–	D
Centaurea montana	Knapweed mountain blue (Mountain bluet)	P	●						●		●	●		1	–
*Chrysanthemum parthenium**	Annual chrysanthemum (Feverfew)	P	●		●						●			–	P1
Crocosmia	Montbretia	Cm				●	●							–	D, A1
Delphinium consolida	Larkspur	Ha	●	●			●		●		●	●		1	A1, P1
Delphinium	Delphiniums	P	●		●		●		●		●	●		3, 1	A1, P1, D
*Dianthus allwoodii**	Pinks	P	●	●	●	●	●	●	●	●	●		●	–	F
*Dianthus barbatus**	Sweet William	P	●				●		●	●	●			–	F
Digitalis	Foxglove	Ha	●	●					●		●	●		1, 3	D
Euphorbia robbiae	Spurge	P											●	2	–
*Freesia**	Freesia	Cm	●	●	●	●	●	●	●	●	●	●		–	D
Gaillardia grandiflora	Blanket flower	P			●	●	●					●		–	D
Geranium grandiflorum	Cranesbill	P	●						●	●	●	●		–	P1
Gerbera jamesonii	Transvaal daisy	P	●	●	●		●				●		●	1	–
Gladiolus	Sword lily	Cm	●	●	●	●	●	●	●	●	●		●	–	D
Helichrysum bracteatum	Strawflower	Ha	●		●	●	●				●			–	A1
Helipterum	Sunray	Ha	●				●				●			–	A1
Hydrangea macrophylla	Hydrangea (French hydrangea)	S	●				●				●	●		5	A2
Hypericum patulum	St. John's wort	S			●									5, 1	–
Iris	Iris	R	●		●				●			●		–	–
*Lathyrus odoratus**	Sweet pea	Ha	●	●			●	●	●	●	●		●	–	P1
Lavandula officinalis	English or common lavender	S							●					–	A1
Leucanthemum vulgare	Ox-eye daisy	P	●		●									–	P1
Leycesteria formosa	Himalayan honeysuckle	S		●					●					1	–
*Lilium longiflorum**	White trumpet lily	B	●											–	–
*Lilium speciosum**	Japanese or showy lily	B					●							–	–
Lilium tigrinum	Tiger lilies	B			●	●	●							–	–
Limonium latifolium	Sea lavender	P	●	●			●		●	●	●	●		–	A1
Limonium sinuatum	Winged statice	Ha	●		●	●			●	●	●	●		–	A1
Lysimachia	Yellow loosestrife	P			●									–	P1
Lythrum salicaria	Purple loosestrife	P							●		●			–	–
*Matthiola incana**	Stock or gillyflower	Bi	●	●			●		●	●	●			1	P1
*Nepeta faassenii**	Catmint	P							●	●		●		–	A1
Nicotania	Flowering tobacco	Ha	●				●		●		●			–	P1
Nigella damascena	Love-in-a-mist	Ha	●	●			●		●	●	●			–	D
Nymphaea	Lotus lily (Water lily)	R	●	●	●		●			●	●	●		–	A1 (sh)

LATIN NAME	COMMON NAME	TYPE	COLOUR											SPECIAL CONDITIONING	PRESERVING
			White	Cream	Yellow	Orange	Red	Brown	Purple	Mauve	Pink	Blue	Green		
Onopordum acanthium	Scotch thistle	P	●				●		●					1	A1 (sh)
Paeonia lactiflora*	Chinese paeony (Common garden peony)	P	●				●		●	●	●			1	G1 (l)
Pelargonium zonale	Geranium	S	●	●	●	●	●		●	●	●			–	P1
Philadelphus*	Mock orange	S	●											5, 1	F
Phlox*	Phlox	P	●				●		●	●	●	●		–	P1
Ranunculus	Buttercup family	P	●		●	●	●				●			–	D(d), P1 (S)
Rosa	Rose	S	●	●	●	●	●	●	●	●			●	5, 1	A1
Rosa polyanthus*	Polyanthus rose	S	●	●	●	●	●	●	●	●	●			5, 1	–
Scabiosa	Pincushion flower	Ha	●		●		●			●	●	●		–	D
Solidago	Golden rod	P			●									5, 1	A1, 2, D
Stachys lanata	Lamb's ears	P							●	●	●			5, 1	G1
Strelitzia reginae	Bird-of-paradise flower	P, G							●		●			–	–
Tanacetum vulgare	Tansy	P			●									1	A1
Trachelium caeruleum*	Common throatwort	P		●					●	●		●		–	–
Typha	Reedmace or bulrush (Cattail)	R						●						–	A2
Veronica	Speedwell	P	●		●		●			●	●			–	–
Viburnum opulus sterile	Snowball bush	S											●	5, 1	–
Xeranthemum	Immortelle	H	●						●	●				–	A1
Zinnia	Zinnia	Ha		●	●	●	●	●	●	●	●	●	●	1	D
AUTUMN															
Aconitum	Monkshood	P	●		●					●				–	A1, A2
Agapanthus	African blue lily	B	●									●		–	D
Amaryllis belladonna*	Belladonna lily	B	●				●				●			–	–
Anemone hupehensis	Japanese anemone	Fr	●						●					–	P1
Antirrhinium	Snapdragon	Ha	●	●	●	●	●	●	●	●			●	1	–
Buddleia*	Butterfly bush	S		●					●					5, 1	–
Callistephus chinensis	China aster or annual aster	Ha	●				●		●	●	●			–	P1(s) D(d)
Campanula glomerata	Clustered bellflower	P	●						●					–	P1
Dahlia	Dahlia	P	●	●	●	●	●	●	●	●	●			–	D
Hydrangea macrophylla	Hydrangea (French hydrangea)	S	●				●			●	●			5	A2
Nepeta faassenii	Catmint	P							●	●		●		–	A1
Nerium oleander	Oleander	S	●	●			●			●				5, 1	P1
Polianthes tuberosa*	Tuberose	R	●									1		–	D
Schizostylis coccinea	Crimson flag or kaffir lily	R									●			–	P1
Sedum	Autumn joy	P									●			–	–
Solidago	Golden rod	P			●									1	A1
WINTER															
Acacia dealbata	Mimosa (Silver wattle)	T			●									5, 1	A1
Jasminum nudiflorum	Winter jasmine	S			●									5	–
Viburnum tinus	Laurustinus	S	●								●			5, 1	–
THROUGHOUT THE YEAR															
Dianthus*	Carnation (pink)	P	●	●	●	●	●		●	●	●			–	F
Chrysanthemum	Chrysanthemum	P, G	●	●	●	●	●	●	●	●	●			5	P1, D
Orchidaceae dendrobium	Singapore orchids	G	●	●	●		●		●	●	●			–	D

FOLIAGE

LATIN NAME	COMMON NAME	TYPE	Light Green	Grey-Green	Yellow-Green	Green	Blue-Green	Dark Green	Grey	Gold	Red-Purple	SPECIAL CONDITIONING	PRESERVING
EVERGREEN/GREENHOUSE													
Adiantum pedatum	Maidenhair fern	G				●						2, 6	P1
Aspidistra elatior	Cast-iron plant	G						●				–	G1
Aucuba japonica	Spotted laurel	S			●							5	–
Ballota pseudodictamus	Ballota	S	●						●			1	G1
Bergenia	Elephant ear	P				●						6	G2
Buxus sempervirens	Box-common	S						●				6	G1
Camellia japonica	Common camellia	S						●				5	G1
Chamaecyparis lawsoniana	Lawson cypress	T					●					5	G1
Chamaecyparis obtusa	Hinoki cypress	T				●				●		5	G1
Chamaerops humilis	European fern palm	T						●				–	A1
Cotoneaster franchetii	Cotoneaster	S		●								5	G1
Cupressus sempervirens	Mediterranean cypress (Italian cypress)	T						●				5	G1
Danaë ralemosa	Alexandrian laurel	S				●						5	G1
Echeveria derenberg	Succulents	G		●								–	–
Eleagnus ebbingei	Oleaster	S		●								5	G1
Eucalyptus gunnii	Cider gum tree	T							●			5	G1
Euonymus japonica	Japanese spindle tree	S						●				5	–
Euonymus fortunei radicans carrieri	Spindles (Spindle tree)	S			●							5	–
Fatsia	False castor oil	S				●						5	G1
Garrya eliptica	Silk tassel bush	S						●				5	G1
Hedera canariensis	Canary Island ivy	Wc						●				5, 6	G1
Hedera helix	Common ivy (English ivy)	Wc						●		●		5, 6	G1
Ilex aquifolium	Holly (English holly)	S						●				5	G1
Jasminium officinale	Summer jasmine	C				●						5, 1	P1
Lagurus ovatus	Hare's tail grass	A	●			●						–	P2
Ligustrum ovalifolium aurea	Golden privet (California privet)	S			●							5	–
Lonicera japonica	Japanese honeysuckle	C			●	●						–	–
Lonicera nitida	Box honeysuckle	S						●				5	–
Magnolia grandiflora	Magnolia bull bay	T						●	●			5	A1, G1
Mahonia japonica	Mahonia (Oregon grape)	S						●				–	G1
Nephrolepis exaltata	Ladder fern	G						●				2, 6	–
Pelargonium crispum	Scented geranium (Lemon geranium)	S						●				–	P1
Phormium tenax	New Zealand flax	P		●				●				–	P1, G1
Pittosporum tenuifolium	Pittosporum	T						●			●	5	G1
Polygonatum hytridum	Solomon's seal	P						●				–	G1
Prunus laurocerasus	English laurel	S						●				5	G1
Rhamnus argentiovariegata	Buckthorn	S		●								5	–
Ruscus aculeatus	Butcher's broom	S						●				5	G1
Ruta graveolens	Rue	P					●					–	P1
Senecio laxifolius	Groundsel	S		●								5	–
Senecio maritima	Groundsel	S							●			5, 1	P1
Skimmia	Skimmia	S						●				5	–

LATIN NAME	COMMON NAME	TYPE	COLOUR									SPECIAL CONDITIONING	PRESERVING
			Light Green	Grey-Green	Yellow-Green	Green	Blue-Green	Dark Green	Grey	Gold	Red-Purple		
Tamarix	Tamarisk	S	●									1	–
Taxus	Yew	T						●				5	G1
Thuja	Arborvitae	T			●							–	G1
Tsuga heterophylla	Western hemlock	T				●						–	–
Vinca major	Greater periwinkle	P						●				–	–

DECIDUOUS

LATIN NAME	COMMON NAME	TYPE	Light Green	Grey-Green	Yellow-Green	Green	Blue-Green	Dark Green	Grey	Gold	Red-Purple	SPECIAL CONDITIONING	PRESERVING
Acer negundo eleganissimum aureomarginatum	Box elder	T	●									5, 4	–
Acer palmatum	Japanese maple	T	●		●							5, 4	–
Acer platanoides	Norway maple	T	●		●							–	–
Alnus glutinosa	Black or common European alder	T				●						5	G1
Arum italicum	Italian arum	R				●						6	–
Athyrium filix femina	Lady fern	P				●						2	A3, P2
Berberis thunbergii	Japanese barberry	S									●	5, 1	–
Betula pendula	Silver birch	T	●									5	G1
Castanea sativa	Sweet or Spanish chestnut	T				●						5	G1
Corylus avellana	Hazel or cob nut	T				●						5	G1
Cotinus coggygria	Smokebush	S									●	5, 1	–
Fagus sylvatica	Beech – common (European beech)	T				●						5	G1
Fagus sylvatica cuprea	Copper beech	T									●	5	G1
Helichrysum angustifolium	Curry plant (White-leaf everlasting)	S							●			–	–
Hosta	Plantain lily	P	●	●		●	●			●		6	G2, A1
Hypericum elatum	St. John's wort	S				●						5	–
Kerria japonica	Jew's mallow (Japanese rose)	S			●							5	–
Lagurus ovatus	Hare's tail grass	A				●						–	A1, G1
*Lippia citriodora**	Lemon-scented verbena	S				●						–	–
Melissa officinalis	Lemon balm	P			●							–	P1
Physocarpus opulifolius	Ninebark	S			●							5, 1	–
Ribes sanguineum	Flowering currant	S	●									5, 1	P1
Salix daphnoides	Violet willow	T				●		●				5	G1
Salix matsudana	Contorted willow (Pekin willow)	T				●						5	G1
Salix sachalinensis serka	Fasciated willow	T		●								5	G1
Sorbus aria	White beam	T		●								5, 1	–
Tilia	Lime or linden	T	●									5, 1	G1
Viburnum	Viburnum (Arrowwood)	S	●									5, 1	–

CONES AND SEEDPODS

LATIN NAME	COMMON NAME	TYPE	Light Green	Grey-Green	Yellow-Green	Green	Blue-Green	Dark Green	Grey	Gold	Red-Purple	SPECIAL CONDITIONING	PRESERVING
Cedrus libani	Cedar of Lebanon	Cn										–	–
Cupressus	Cypress	Cn										–	–
Delonix regia	Flame tree	Sp										–	–
Dipsacus fullonum	Teasel	Sp										–	–
Nigella damascena	Love-in-a-mist	Sp										–	–
Onopordum acanthium	Scotch thistle	Sp										–	–
Picea orientalis	Oriental spruce	C										–	–
Pinus nigra maritima	Corsican pine	Cn										–	–
Pinus pinea	Umbrella pine	Cn										–	–
Pinus wallicheana	Himalayan pine	C										–	–

HALLS
AND STAIRWAYS

Opposite: the warm colours of this triangular hall arrangement welcome guests and brighten a neglected area.

Flowers & foliage:
CRIMSON AND WHITE STARGAZER LILIES, CRIMSON SEA LAVENDER, DEEP ORANGE TIGER LILIES, RED, PINK AND WHITE SWEET WILLIAM, RUST SPRAY CHRYSANTHEMUMS, PURPLE SINGAPORE ORCHIDS, DARK RED ORNAMENTAL ONIONS.

Mechanics:
FLORIST'S FOAM, CHICKEN WIRE, TAPE, DEEP BOWL.

Right: this preserved arrangement is ideal for the hallway and tones with the natural wood tones of the room. The Hogarth curve breaks the straight lines made by the floorboards and walls.

Flowers & foliage:
YELLOW STRAWFLOWERS, YELLOW ACHILLEA, PURPLE STATICE, GOLDEN BROWN SCOTCH THISTLE, CREAM SEA LAVENDER, GLYCERINED CREAM RUSCUS, PURPLE EUCALYPTUS, GREY-BROWN LAMB'S EARS CALYXES, DARK BROWN LAUREL LEAVES.

Mechanics: FOAM HOLDER, DRY FLORIST'S FOAM, CHICKEN WIRE, TAPE.

A COLOURFUL DISPLAY OF FLOWERS in the hallway provides a warm welcome for visitors. Equally it is a pleasant surprise to come across an arrangement in the corner of a stairway or in a narrow passage.

When planning the design remember that many halls lack space for a large arrangement; they can be cool and draughty near the outer door and are often fairly dark in the daytime as well as at night. You can overcome the problem of lack of space and colour in a narrow hall or passage by arranging flowers on a shelf or, where space allows, using a curve on the stairs for a small pedestal arrangement. Or simply place a wide, shallow bowl of flowers on a hall table – this is best for a larger hall. A low bowl is not likely to be knocked over by people passing by and will hold plenty of water, thereby providing humidity for the plant material, which transpires quickly in draughty conditions.

Above: the flowers and foliage for artificial arrangements are available from florists and some garden centres.

Flowers & foliage:

ALL SILK PALE PINK AND BROWN ROSES, CREAM LILIES, GYPSOPHILA, GREEN ROSE FOLIAGE, FERNS, LARGE VARIEGATED LEAVES.

Mechanics:

FOAM HOLDER, DRY FLORIST'S FOAM, TAPE.

LONG-LASTING ARRANGEMENTS

These are ideal for the hallway – an area of the home which is passed through yet which will most certainly be highlighted by an attractive arrangement.

Dried or preserved arrangements are ideal as they last almost indefinitely. Precisely because they do last so long, it is important not to leave the arrangement to become tired and dusty-looking. You can purchase dried material at most florists and garden centres, or, as indicated on pages 14–15, you can grow and preserve or glean your own dry material from the countryside.

As no water is required, you can place the stems at any angle or cross them high in a modern arrangement for contrasting line direction. You can also wire single leaves into sprays, create 'flowers' by sticking honesty seedpods into a wired fir cone, and cut, stick, tie or wire together preserved material to create different shapes or forms.

Plant material preserved by the glycerine method has generally rather blurred, subtle colours, so good use of different textures is essential to give impact. Shiny mahonia (Oregon grape) and laurel leaves and a contrasting base or container will help give vitality to the design. Moreover, if you add rough-textured dried material such as yellow yarrow (*Achillea* spp.), cream bells of Ireland (*Molucella laevis*) or green hydrangeas (*Hydrangea* spp.) to glycerined beech (*Fagus* spp.) leaves in a shiny brass jug, you will

This arrangement relies on a range of foliage with just a few flowers, and makes novel use of an old wash bowl.

Flowers & foliage:
PALE PINK PERENNIAL GERANIUMS, GREEN SOLOMON'S SEAL LEAVES, EUONYMUS 'EMERALD AND GOLD', EUONYMUS 'SILVER QUEEN', VARIEGATED BOX, GOLDEN LEMON BALM, GOLDEN (CALIFORNIA) PRIVET, VARIEGATED HOSTA LEAVES, PALE GOLD PHYSOCARPUS LEAVES.

Mechanics: FOAM HOLDER, FLORIST'S FOAM, TAPE, PLASTIC BOWL PLACED INSIDE THE WASH BOWL.

create an exciting and texturally interesting arrangement.

Modern designs with their minimal plant material should have very strong textural contrasts to make the design exciting. A few contrasting groups of textures are more effective than several textures dotted throughout the arrangement. Dried flowers, herbs and grasses massed in a wicker basket might be attractive for a country cottage; a swirl of driftwood, large, smooth leaves and bold seed heads in a tall, slim

container would complement modern furnishings, while an elegant pedestal with the flowing glycerined leaves, bells of Ireland and sea holly (*Eryngium* spp.) and dried flowers of yarrow and hydrangea already described would look striking in a large hall.

Mixed material
During the winter-time it is not always easy to find foliage to go with fresh flowers, so this is where a supply of leaves glycerined in the summer or purchased from the florist will come

*A hanging arrangement
for a wall light or candle
sconce.*

Flowers & foliage:
YELLOW ALSTROEMERIA
AND ROSES, GOLDEN
PRIVET, GREY-GREEN
BALLOTA, VARIEGATED
CANARY ISLAND IVY.

Mechanics:
BRASS-COLOURED
CANDLE CUP, PLASTIC
FOAM HOLDER, FLORIST'S
FOAM.

in useful as they mix happily with fresh flowers. It is a good idea to dip the glycerined stems in varnish so that the glycerine does not leak out into the water. Alternatively combine silk or polyester flowers with fresh or preserved foliage to create an attractive arrangement.

ARRANGEMENTS WITH FEW FLOWERS

There are several ways in which a few flowers or foliage can be used to make an effective design.

Pot et fleur

This is a group of house-plants in one container with a few fresh flowers interspersed.

Use a container such as a large bowl and leave the plants in their pots or remove them and plant in the container, leaving space for a small dish in which to place the cut flowers. When they wilt, you can replace them with fresh ones, perhaps of a different variety and colour.

A *pot et fleur* is long-lasting and economical as the plants need not be replaced for some time, and just a few flowers among the plants can look very dramatic. Plants grouped in this way also have more impact than scattered single plants and they make their own moist micro-climate, which encourages growth and helps to counteract the drying effect of central heating.

● *Selecting the plants:* select healthy-looking plants with no wilting leaves, pests or signs of disease. The potting soil or compost should be damp, no roots should protrude from the base of the pot and you should be able to see young buds or shoots.

When removing the plants from their pots, select those which need the same amount of water, temperature, light and humidity. When selecting the plants in the shop, group them to see how well they go together. You will need a tall, slender plant for height, a bold-leaved one for the centre, some which trail prettily over the edge and one or two with medium-sized leaves as fillers. Bowls consisting entirely of green leaves are very unexciting; select a few variegated plants and one or two of a different colour for drama. You can combine plants to suit the colour scheme of the room and use the flowers to echo the colour of nearby furnishings or ornaments.

● *Design:* When constructing a *pot et fleur*, the same elements and principles of design apply as in flower arranging. The finished shape of the design should be pleasing, plants with variety or contrast in form, colour and texture should be chosen; they should also be in scale both with each other and with the container.

The container should suit the setting and should not be so dominant that it detracts from the plants. It must, of course, be watertight and at least 4 inches (10 cm) deep to hold the plants and potting compost and to allow sufficient depth for watering. If the plants are to remain in their pots the container should be deeper than the pots. China or pottery bowls, lined baskets and lined wooden or metal bowls and boxes all make attractive containers.

● *Suggestions:* small flowering plants such as African violets (*Saintpaulia ionantha*), polyanthus (*Primula* x *polyantha*) or cyclamen (*Cyclamen* spp.); driftwood to give height, small pieces of bark, stones or moss to fill in the spaces; attractive rocks, coral, shells or sea fan.

PLANTS SUITABLE FOR HALLS

The plants described below are fairly tolerant of the dull lighting and cool conditions found in some halls, and combine well in decorative groups.

Dumb cane
(Dieffenbachia exotica)
An attractive, compact plant with large leaves splashed with creamy white blotches.

Kangaroo vine
(Cissus antarctica)
A tall vine-like climber which can be trained and gives height to a group of plants.

Sweetheart vine, *or heart-leaf philodendron* (Philodendron scandens)
This plant can be trained up a pole or a frame; it has green, glossy, heart-shaped leaves.

Spider plant
(Chlorophytum comosum)
This house-plant is very easy to grow and look after and has long, narrow green and white leaves. New plants are formed at the end of long stems.

Bird's-nest fern
(Asplenium nidus)
A glossy dark green plant with long, leathery leaves with wavy edges.

Silver lace fern
(Pteris ensiformis victoriae)
A compact fern with silvery leaves edged in dark green.

Snake plant
(Sansevieria trifasciata)
A fairly tall plant with long, succulent leaves of dark green and grey.

Peace lily
(Spathyphyllum clevelandis)
A handsome, decorative plant with glossy, pointed leaves on slender stems and with white flowers.

Ivy
(Hedera helix)
An attractive plant with dark green, ivy-like leaves.

This richly coloured hanging arrangement is easily created by inserting florist's foam in the letter rack and is ideally suited to a narrow hall where there is sufficient head-room.

Flowers & foliage:
PEACH ROSES, CORAL ALSTROEMERIA, PURPLE SINGAPORE ORCHIDS, DEEP RED PINKS, PINK SINGAPORE ORCHIDS, GREEN AND WHITE *LEYCESTERIA FORMOSA*, PEACH ACHILLEA, LADDER FERN, IVY LEAVES, GREY-GREEN BALLOTA, GREY BUDS OF *SENECIO MARITIMA* (GROUNDSEL), *COTONEASTER FRANCHETII*.

Mechanics:
FLORIST'S FOAM.

FOLIAGE AND FLOWERS

An arrangement consisting mainly of fresh long-lasting foliage can have a few flowers stepped down through the centre. As these flowers die, you can change the water and add new flowers.

LONG-LASTING LEAVES

These are usually evergreen. Very young, fresh foliage would not be suitable for a hall as it might wilt in the draughts. The following plants have long-lasting leaves: spotted laurel (*Aucuba japonica*), Mexican orange (*Choisya ternata*), cypress (*Cupressus*), oleaster (*eleagnus ebbingei*), false castor-oil plant (*Fatsia japonica*), ivy, mature plantain lily (*Hosta* spp.), iris (*Iris* spp.), mahonia (*Mahonia japonica*), New Zealand flax (*Phormium tenaf*), *Viburnum tinus* and arum lily, or calla lily, (*Zantedeschia*).

SIMPLE OUTLINE DESIGNS

Bare branches, catkins, pussy willow, reedmaces, cattails or bulrushes (*Typha* spp.), honeysuckle vine (*Lonicera* spp.) or curled cane in a simple container can form the outline of a basic design.

Add weight to the base of the arrangement by using bracket fungi, stones, shells or fir cones or some large fresh or glycerined leaves. You can then simply leave the basic outline in place, adding fresh flowers as necessary.

FLOWERS TO COMPLEMENT A PICTURE

Very often there are pictures hanging above a hall table, and an arrangement standing on a table beneath it can be most attractive if it complements the picture in some way. A woodland scene might be complemented by an arrangement on a natural wood base with ferns, fungi, driftwood and a few simple flowers. While a bright, cubist picture might be enhanced by a bold modern design using one or two of the colours in the picture. A painting of ballet dancers would be well co-ordinated with an arrangement containing plenty of swirling movement to echo that of the dancers.

HOLIDAY MEMORIES

A hall table is a welcoming place to display holiday souvenirs accompanied by a group of flowers in a unified whole. An appropriate base links the group and also makes it easier to move about for dusting. Do assess souvenirs for size, colour, style and texture before deciding on the type of arrangement.

A group of shells and coral from the Bahamas, for instance, would probably look more attractive than a single small shell, and the colour and satin-like sheen on the inside of the shells could be echoed in the petals of flowers within the arrangement. A small, colourful figurine of a Spanish dancer could be raised and placed towards the front of the design to give it more prominence. There are endless possibilities – use your own holiday souvenirs for inspiration.

Holiday souvenirs can provide unusual accessories. Here a wooden base appropriately links the wood carving with nearby ornaments and the piano in this Bohemian setting.

Flowers & foliage:
CRIMSON AND WHITE STARGAZER LILIES, GREY-GREEN *HOSTA SIBOLDIANA* LEAVES.

Mechanics: LARGE, HEAVY PINHOLDER.

THE
LIVING-ROOM

*T*HE LIVING-ROOM, whether an elegant drawing-room or a comfortable sitting-room, is a place for relaxing and where you tend to take in your surroundings. You probably spend more waking hours here than in any other room.

As it is the place where you spend time in the evening, the living-room is usually warmer than other rooms and plant material tends to transpire at a rapid rate. Warmth also intensifies the perfume of flowers, so very heavily perfumed flowers, such as some lilies (*Lilium* spp.), are not recommended as the effect could be rather overpowering. Flowers with a delicate perfume such as violets (*Viola* spp.) or sweet peas (*Lathyrus odoratus*) give freshness to a living-room.

Three ways of enhancing a cottage living room.

Flowers & foliage:
LEFT: CREAM LILIES, PINK AND YELLOW SPRAY CARNATIONS, MAUVE COMMON THROATWORT, CREAM ROSES, PINK ALSTROEMERIA AND PHLOX, EUONYMUS 'EMERALD AND GOLD', GOLDEN PRIVET, MONTBRETIA LEAVES, BERGENIA LEAVES, WEIGELA LEAVES, *VIBURNUM GRANDIFLORUM* LEAVES.
FOREGROUND: PINK GERANIUM, PINK AND YELLOW ALSTROEMERIA.
RIGHT: PINK ROSES AND LILY, YELLOW RANUNCULUS, CREAM SINGAPORE ORCHIDS, MAUVE COMMON THROATWORT.

Mechanics:
LEFT: PINHOLDER, NYLON JERSEY, FLORIST'S FOAM, CHICKEN WIRE.
RIGHT: CHICKEN WIRE.

A fresh approach for a living-room: the striking colours of the arrangement co-ordinate with the furnishings.

Flowers & foliage:
FOREGROUND: ARUM LILY (CALLA LILLY), GREEN GODDESS, PINK AMARYLLIS, BLUE BELLFLOWER AND SCABIUS, YELLOW-GREEN HOSTA LEAVES, GREY-GREEN *HOSTA SIEBOLDIANA* LEAVES.

BACKGROUND: BIRD-OF-PARADISE FLOWERS, DEEP BLUE LARKSPUR, BIRD OF PARADISE LEAVES, LARGE ARUM LILY LEAVES.

BACKGROUNDS AND SETTINGS

Always try to complement beautiful furniture with your arrangements as well, but make sure that they do not hide it. For instance, when designing a summer arrangement in the fireplace you might include both the colours of the ornaments on the mantelpiece and in the picture above it, plus some of the fruits and flowers in the carving of the fire surround. A flowing asymmetric design within a carved wooden box on a low table with part of the open lid showing is another idea, while some shining, brown, preserved laurel (*Laurus* spp.) and mahonia, or Oregon grape, (*Mahonia* spp.) leaves and fresh flowers would complement an old oak chest. You could also use a container with a pedestal base to raise the flowers above an antique polished table.

Flowers can also be used to divert the eye from an unattractive feature or to decorate an otherwise bare area. Generally, one or two larger designs look better than a disarray of several smaller ones, which tend to give an unco-ordinated and spotted effect.

The tables, shelves and mantelpiece in the living-room generally hold many objects, ornaments, lamps, ashtrays, a tea-tray, glasses or books. When planning your flower arrangement remember to leave space for all of these to avoid a cluttered look and any damage or accidents to the arrangement.

A selection of anemones, ranunculus and ivy in a low posy arrangement suitable for a coffee table.

Flowers & foliage:
RED ANEMONES, CREAM ANEMONES WITH PINK CENTRES, WHITE RANUNCULUS, LARGE WILD IVY LEAVES.

Mechanics:
PINHOLDER.

This L-shaped
arrangement is enhanced
by dappled sunlight. The
design gives equal weight
to foliage and flowers. The
foliage is reminiscent of
the view outside, while the
blue irises provide a link
with the container.

Flowers & foliage:
WHITE CHERRY BLOSSOM,
LIME GREEN *EUPHORBIA
ROBBIAE*, BLUE IRIS, PALE
GREEN STINKING
HELLEBORE, LAUREL,
MONTBRETIA FLOWERS,
BERGENIA LEAVES, BLUE-
GREEN WESTERN
HEMLOCK, VARIEGATED
PERIWINKLE.

Mechanics: METAL
FOAM HOLDER, FLORIST'S
FOAM, CHICKEN WIRE,
TAPE.

The rustic charm of a fireplace can be emphasized using an elegant traditional arrangement. An arrangement should not fill the surrounding space completely.

Flowers & foliage:

SILK CREAM PEACH LILIES AND LARGE ROSES, PEACH SPRAY ROSES, DUSKY PINK POPPIES, SILK ROSE LEAVES, FRESH BLUE-GREEN WESTERN HEMLOCK, JAPANESE ANEMONE LEAVES, GREEN HONESTY SEEDPODS, *COTONEASTER FRANCHETII.*

Mechanics:

PINHOLDER, NYLON JERSEY MATERIAL, CHICKEN WIRE, TAPE.

SIZE AND SCALE

When you have decided where to stand your flower arrangement, you will need to think about its eventual size. Try to visualize the space as a three-dimensional block with the wall and existing furnishings or ornaments as its boundary. The flowers should not fill this imagined block completely as this would give a crowded effect; space both around it as well as within the design is needed. On the other hand, a flower arrangement that is too small for the space will not have any impact.

The space is also limited by the height of the ceiling and any picture which may hang above the design. Since a picture is a feature on its own, the flowers should not hide it; you should, in fact, place them either below or to the side of the picture. You can put a bare corner or wall to good use by filling it with a larger design – perhaps raised from the ground or on a column or a pedestal.

Your next move is to select a container and plant material of the correct scale. Remember that large, bold designs need a heavier container and big flowers and leaves, whereas small designs need dainty plant material and small containers.

SHAPE AND FORM

The area or space in which you wish to place an arrangement helps to suggest the finished shape of the design. Sometimes the shape of the table or base for the design will be the deciding factor. A small, round, free-standing table might have a fairly low, posy-shaped arrangement which can be viewed from all round, a long, slim design would complement a rectangular table, or the curve of a natural wood base could be repeated in the plant material.

For any low table arrangement, there should be sufficient space on the table, which may well be crowded with crockery, books or magazines.

A narrow alcove calls for a slender, vertical design: a dramatic idea in a modern room is to combine a cylindrical container, a rosette of rhododendron (*Rhododendron* spp.) leaves placed low down, two brilliant pink gerbera (*Gerbera jamesonii*) and a soaring branch. In more traditional surroundings a slim, symmetrical triangle or a Byzantine cone in a stemmed container would be a most suitable arrangement for the alcove.

A design for one end of a shelf or a mantelpiece could take the shape of an asymmetric triangle with longer plant material flowing over the end of the shelf. Another shape which looks well on a shelf is an elegant S-shaped (Hogarth) curve arranged in a raised container. If you wish to place the design in the centre of the mantelpiece, then a low symmetrical triangular design might suit this space.

A traditional design to be displayed against a wall to one side of the fireplace could also be in the shape of an asymmetric triangle, a shape which calls for more creativity than the more ordinary symmetrical arrangement. Modern designs can also be raised, the most suitable pedestal being a slender cylinder or a tall, four-sided column.

COLOUR SCHEMES

The colour and style of the furnishings in your living-room are important factors in selecting a colour scheme for your arrangements. Use the colours of flowers and containers to tone with the existing colour scheme of a room by the subtle use of varying shades, or to provide dramatic contrasts, particularly in a stark modern living-room with plain furnishings.

Most furnishings and *objets d'art* are semi-permanent fixtures since they and their colours are not often changed. You can introduce new colours into the room with flowers and change them frequently at little cost. While many people tend to choose flowers of the same colour to decorate their rooms ('safe' colours which they know will blend with the furnishings), it is challenging to introduce a different colour scheme and this is bound to cause comment. If you frequently opt for a particular shade of pink, try adding more tints and tones of this colour, or perhaps a little mauve and cream with grey foliage or even an all-green arrangement. You do not need to pick or buy a mass of flowers to bring a touch of colour into your living-room. A vase placed at eye level and containing a single choice rose from the garden or an exotic spray of orchids can give much pleasure. You can also use single flowers to highlight a group of objects, providing a colourful and textural contrast.

Some living-rooms are very colourful with patterned furnishings; in these settings, arrangements of flowers in tints and shades of one colour would have more impact than a bunch of mixed colours. The effect is most harmonious when the colours of the flowers pick out one of the colours in the furnishings. Other rooms are decorated predominantly in tints, tones and shades of one colour. If your chosen colour scheme is blue, you could select orange, its complementary colour, for a dramatic and warm arrangement or, on a hot summer's day, a bowl of white roses might provide the required cool effect.

If you place more than one arrangement in a room, flowers containing some colour relationship in each design will provide a harmonious effect.

TEXTURE

As already indicated on pages 29–30, the texture of flowers, containers, bases and setting should all harmonize. A glazed white porcelain vase on a natural brick fireplace would introduce a jarring note, while an unglazed pottery container would look much more harmonious. Dark brown, shiny, glycerined mahonia would repeat the gleam on a polished mahogany table, the satin petals of roses (*Rosa* spp.) in a small bowl would complement the texture of cups and saucers on a coffee table, the varied textures in a dried arrangement show up well against a plain wall and the velvety petals of pansies (*Viola* spp.) would be ideal placed near a velvet upholstered chair.

In general, smooth, dainty-looking textures suit traditional settings, while rough, shiny, bold textures complement the uncluttered lines of a modern room.

FLOWERS ON PEDESTALS

If your living-room is large enough to accommodate a pedestal, this is a most attractive way to display an arrangement. It stands in isolation, has a certain sense of drama and should be allowed to take centre stage in its setting. Do take particular care, however, to ensure that it is not so overpowering that it dominates the room

SPRING PEDESTAL

WHAT YOU WILL NEED

Flowers & foliage: WHITE CHERRY BLOSSOM, CREAM TIGER LILIES, YELLOW SPRAY CARNATIONS, PALE YELLOW SPRAY DAISY CHRYSANTHEMUMS, DARK MAUVE ROSES, PALE MAUVE LILAC, PALE MAUVE SPRAY DAISY CHRYSANTHEMUMS, DOUBLE YELLOW TULIPS, SILVERY WHITEBEAM, PALE GREEN LIME, LARGE FATSIA LEAVES.

Other materials: TALL PEDESTAL, CONTAINER, FLORIST'S FOAM, CHICKEN WIRE, FLORIST'S TAPE.

1 *cut foam to fit container and leave to soak. Tuck chicken wire down between blocks and container; tape in place. Insert straight stem of whitebeam 1/3 inch (8 mm) from back; insert long pieces and fine stems of lime in side and large fatsia in centre.*

2 *add sprays of white cherry blossom, keeping within defined outline. Place some blossom at back for depth and weight. Place one lily in centre and rest in a stepped vertical line. Insert spray carnations to give outline and yellow spray chrysanthemums to fill centre.*

3 *position roses in a vertical line, then fill in with pale mauve lilac and a few mauve daisy chrysanthemums towards centre. Fill gaps with cherry blossom and foliage.*

The finishing touch: *check arrangement looks full all around. Add five deeper yellow double tulips to strengthen colour. Fill container with water. Large arrangements require filling up with water daily.*

STAGE *1*

STAGE *2*

STAGE *3*

to the exclusion of everything else. Make sure that it is in scale with the setting and that, as with all arrangements, it harmonizes with the style, architecture and furnishings of the room.

Flower arrangements, *pot et fleur* and feature house-plants can all be elevated on pedestals. They should stand against the wall, preferably with a plain background with plenty of space either side of the design.

Pedestals come in many shapes and sizes: Victorian stands in fluted polished mahogany, smooth marble columns, heavy stone columns, antique carved stands, carved figurines supporting a base for the flowers, very tall, slim tables, wrought iron in many forms and elegant reproduction Grecian columns.

ARRANGING FLOWERS ON A PEDESTAL

Some pedestals have their own built-in container, others have a stand at the top on which a bowl, urn or other container can be placed. Actual balance is a very important consideration with pedestal design because the arrangement is usually placed against a wall, and most of the weight of the mass of plant material will consequently be to the front of the design; unless the mechanics are, therefore, very carefully secured the whole arrangement will topple over. The receptacle should contain a very heavy pinholder secured to the base of the container with florist's fixing clay. A square of nylon jersey material should be placed over the pinholder to facilitate the removal of the florist's foam when the flowers have died. Then place soaked green florist's foam covered with 2 inch (5 cm) mesh chicken wire and securely tied down or fixed with florist's tape in the container. This provides further support and helps to hold the florist's foam together in the container. These preparations are vitally important because it is all too easy – and quite heartbreaking – for a carefully nurtured pedestal to crash to the ground.

As pedestal designs are usually fairly tall, a few pieces of plant material may need to be lifted by the use of cones or orchid tubes, as described on page 13. Do remember to secure the tubes firmly on a cane and to hide them with plant material. Remember as well to fill the orchid tubes with water when you are replenishing the water in the main container.

Since a pedestal arrangement is larger than most designs, you will need taller and bolder plant material so that you will achieve the correct scale between the tall container and the flowers. As these arrangements can be expensive you can use either more foliage than flowers or supplement fresh flowers with seasonally correct

Opposite: accessories should suit both the setting and arrangement and need to harmonize in scale, colour and texture. This modern arrangement complements the figurines at its side.

Flowers & foliage:
WHITE CASABLANCA LILY.

Mechanics:
PINHOLDER.

artificial ones. If you do not already own a pedestal and wish to purchase or construct one, take a good look at the place where it will stand and the style and colour scheme of your room first. Remember that the pedestal does not always have to carry a flower arrangement; it can look equally attractive bearing an interesting pot plant, lamp or suitable ornament. The main advantage of a pedestal is that whatever is placed on the stand can be seen and enjoyed from all parts of the room, whether you are standing up or sitting down.

FLOWERS WITH FIGURINES

Figurines can take the form of various human figures, with styles varying widely from a fat bronze cherub to the cool elegance of a Spanish Lladro lady. They can also take the form of animals, birds and mythical figures. Among your ornaments you probably have some kind of

figurine already or perhaps a pair of statuettes; why not give them new prominence with a complementary flower arrangement linking the whole group with a harmonious base?

There are many ways of styling an arrangement. For example, you could stand a pair of Dresden porcelain figurines on a velvet base and surround each figure with dainty flowers. Use your imagination – you could link the dainty flowers to form an archway between the lover and his lass. Alternatively, set nymphs in a natural-looking woodland scene using a natural wood base and small-leaved forest foliage; or place a carved wooden Chinese fisherman amongst fine, brown, preserved foliage, russet and gold chrysanthemums and a simple arrangement of iris and arum leaves in a low onyx bowl. The bowl might also enhance the colours and textures of a pair of china birds standing beside it on a soft, green silk-covered base.

Right: the use of figurines, in this case white marble muses, provides a colour link with the white gladioli and phlox. The figurines are carefully placed close to and facing the flowers, making them an integral part of the design.

Flowers & foliage:
WHITE GLADIOLI, WHITE PHLOX, CREAM SPRAY CARNATIONS, BLUE DELPHINIUMS, BLUE CATMINT, PURPLE STATICE, JEW'S MALLOW, VARIEGATED HOSTA LEAVES, FORSYTHIA FOLIAGE.

THE DINING-ROOM

A HARMONIOUS ARRANGEMENT OF FLOWERS on a dining-room or buffet table, complementing the general colour scheme and shape of both table and room, can make a meal more stimulating, whether a family lunch or formal occasion.

BASIC CONSIDERATIONS

Unless your dining-room is ultra modern or very ornate and full of antique furniture, basic points of style to consider for arrangements will not vary very much. Apart from colour schemes and shapes, consider also whether the flowers are for every day, an informal gathering of friends, a formal dinner party or a special celebration. Each occasion differs greatly and requires a different style of arrangement, container, plant material, a different colour scheme and table setting.

Much of the space on a table is occupied by place settings, drinking glasses and mats for vegetable tureens and so on, so a table arrangement should therefore co-ordinate with these items without dominating them. Equally, an arrangement should not be so large and high that you are unable to see the people on the opposite side of the table. A fairly low design or a tall one in a slim-stemmed container such as a candlestick enables the diners to see and talk to each other across the table. Usually the diners are seated all around the table, so your design should look attractive from the sides as well as when

When using a colourful table-cloth, plant material should pick out one or two of the colours. This yellow arrangement placed in a neutral container also complements the design of the cloth.

Flowers & foliage:
YELLOW SPRAY CARNATIONS, ROSES AND FREESIAS, WHITE PHYSOCARPUS FLOWERS WITH LIME-COLOURED LEAVES, VARIEGATED UNDULATING HOSTA LEAVES.

Mechanics: FLORIST'S FOAM, TAPE.

seen from above. When you have finished your arrangement it is a good idea to view it from a seated position to check that it looks good from this angle. Round or oval arrangements match similarly shaped tables, while a slim, oval design, a garland or two to three small arrangements in a line might suit a rectangular table.

The flowers on a dining-table are both very near to the seated diners, who will be looking at the arrangement for a long time and in close proximity to the food. You should therefore groom the plant material particularly well, wash any dusty foliage and remove any damaged leaves, and ensure the flowers are in perfect condition and not infested with insects. Greenfly, earwigs or caterpillars crawling over the flowers or table should not form part of the décor!

When diners are seated all around the table the most logical position for the arrangement is in the centre. When only two sides of the table are occupied you could place it at one or both free sides or, if it is a crescent-shaped design, at one end of an oval table to repeat the curve of the table. There are numerous possibilities and it can be challenging to try a new style and shape of arrangement – but practise first for important dinner parties.

Do also bear in mind that strongly perfumed flowers and leaves are not suitable for a dinner table because their scent could conflict with the smell of the food. The curry plant, or white-leaf everlasting (*Helichrysum angustifolium*), for instance, gives off a very strong smell and is only suitable if curry is being served.

COLOUR AND HARMONY

The colours in an arrangement should repeat or contrast with one or two of the colours already present in the china or the table linen. An arrangement of dainty pink and white flowers would complement white china covered in tiny pink rose buds; lime green candles and foliage with white flowers and china would look striking on a royal blue cloth and a deep pink cloth covered with a white lace over-cloth would be an elegant setting for an arrangement of paler pink flowers in a silver candelabra.

The surface of the table might also be a source of inspiration; a natural pine table set with light-coloured rush mats, blue and white china and a basket of blue hyacinths (*Hyacinthus* spp.)

and pale yellow and white narcissus (*Narcissus* hybrids) would be reminiscent of spring in the country. An arrangement of golden-yellow roses with the brownish red foliage of *Berberis thunbergii atropurpurea* and the smoke bush, or European beech, (*Cotinus coggygria*) would harmonize in colour and texture with a dark brown polished wood table. A stark, black table would look good with a design consisting of white gerberas, lime green fruit and foliage and a touch of yellow to sharpen the colour impact of the arrangement. You should also consider the form of lighting when deciding upon a particular arrangement, since colours can vary quite dramatically in different types of lighting.

Flowers in a Terracotta Vase *by Jan van Huysum (1682–1749). The warm colours of the vase and red and orange flowers contrast with the cool blue and white flowers and green grapes in the foreground. A similar combination of fruit and flowers would be particularly appropriate for a dinner party.*

Right: a formal dinner party arrangement using soft-coloured exotic flowers, under the glow of candlelight; the candelabra adds a further touch of elegance. Do remember to have a trial run before attempting a new design.

Flowers & foliage:

WHITE SINGAPORE ORCHIDS, PINK SPRAY ROSES, PINK SPRAY CARNATIONS, BLUE-GREEN EUCALYPTUS AND WESTERN HEMLOCK, GREY-GREEN SENECIO 'SUNSHINE', ROSE LEAVES.

Mechanics: CANDLE CUPS, PLASTIC FOAM HOLDERS, FLORIST'S FOAM, TAPE, CANDLES WITH COCKTAIL STICK (TOOTHPICK) 'LEGS'.

Opposite: a tall arrangement in a silver container with a raised silver base leaves room for surrounding ornaments. The candlelight adds warmth and elegance to a sophisticated arrangement.

Flowers & foliage:

WHITE SPRAY CARNATIONS, CREAM STOCKS, WHITE ROSES, WHITE SPIRAEA 'BRIDAL WREATH', CREAM SWEET PEAS, WHITE BOUVARDIA, *VIBURNUM TINUS* LEAVES, GREEN HOSTA LEAVES.

Mechanics: FLORIST'S FOAM, CHICKEN WIRE, TAPE, GLASS DISH THAT FITS INSIDE THE SILVER CONTAINER.

BUFFET TABLES

Food for a buffet should be placed on a sideboard
or on a buffet table in the centre of the room.
Generally, arrangements for buffet tables need to
be tall so that they can be seen above the display
of food, but should not impede the way of people
collecting their meal. They should have a firm
base so that they are not knocked over. The
width and overall size of the arrangement will be
determined by the available space. If you have
room you could present a buffet arrangement as a
dramatic part of the spread. Driftwood,
pheasants' feathers, beech leaves, a swirl of tartan
material and some flowers to pick out a colour in
the tartan could be particularly appropriate on

New Year's Eve. If you have less room, a tall, slim
column would lift an arrangement and prevent it
from interfering with the food. If you place the
buffet table in the centre of the room you will
need to view the arrangement from all around;
this means that you will need additional plant
material.

DINNER PARTIES

An informal dinner calls for an attractively set
table and a pretty centrepiece. You can afford to
be bolder with the colour combinations and
contrasts than you can for a more formal dinner.
One idea might be to gain inspiration from the
Dutch seventeenth century paintings and include

DINNER PARTY

WHAT YOU WILL NEED

Flowers & foliage: ORANGE SPRAY CARNATIONS, RUST-COLOURED SPIDER CHRYSANTHEMUMS, RUST-COLOURED DOUBLE SPRAY CHRYSANTHEMUMS, PALE YELLOW SPRAY CARNATIONS, CALIFORNIAN LILAC LEAVES, EUONYMUS 'EMERALD AND GOLD', EUONYMUS 'SILVER QUEEN', CANARY ISLAND IVY LEAVES, VARIEGATED IVY LEAVES.

Other materials: FLORIST'S FOAM, CONTAINER ON STEM, HEAVY METAL FOAMHOLDER, FLORIST'S FIXING CLAY, COCKTAIL STICKS (TOOTHPICKS), PAIR OF TONING CANDLES, TRANSPARENT TAPE, SMALL TURNTABLE.

1 cut foam to fit container and to protrude 1 inch (2.5 cm) above rim. Fix foam holder in container with florist's fixing clay. Soak foam until fully charged and press on to foam holder. Tape three cocktail stick (toothpick) 'legs' to each candle with the 'legs' protruding below the candle. Insert both candles into top of foam, one slightly higher than the other. Place container on turntable. Place 2 pieces Californian lilac of equal length into opposite sides of foam and shorter pieces in remaining 2 sides. Place increasingly shorter pieces of both types of euonymus inside lilac 'frame' and large ivy leaves in centre.

2 make sure that no stems are touching the table. Add buds of orange spray carnations at the outer tips, working inwards with the more open flowers. Add rust-coloured open spider chrysanthemums to centre and place some half-opened buds of spray chrysanthemums beside them.

3 include pale yellow spray carnations in the arrangement.

The finishing touch: place arrangement on table and examine from a sitting position. Check all-round view of arrangement. If necessary, add a few more sprays of euonymus 'emerald and gold' to fill arrangement out and to hide florist's foam. Fill container with water.

STAGE *1*

STAGE *2*

STAGE *3*

fruit. (*See* illustration page 71.) Similarly you could use candles either as an integral part of the arrangement or separately in a candlestick. They should harmonize with the flowers and foliage and should not be in such a dominant colour that the eye is drawn to them to the exclusion of the rest of the table setting. A piece of your dinner service, such as a soup bowl, round or oval dishes in a pale shade of green or the colour of one of the flowers and slightly raised containers are all suitable for an informal dinner-table arrangement. You can place the flowers directly on to the cloth, on one of the mats used for the place settings or on a material-covered oval or round base. Do, however, avoid any flowers or foliage touching the surface of the table as water may be syphoned out and mark the table.

Formal dinner parties should be elegant occasions, where the décor, table setting and flowers all harmonize and complement the food being served. Use fine linen, damask or lace cloths, napkins or mats in soft colours. A plain, strong-coloured cloth can be muted by adding an over-cloth in cream or white lace.

For a formal occasion the arrangement needs to be more exotic than for an informal one. Use soft-coloured, pretty flowers such as orchids (*Cymbidium* hybrid, for example), roses (*Rosa* spp.), carnations (*Dianthus* spp.) and freesia (*Freesia* spp.) with a froth of gypsophila (*Gypsophila* spp.) for lightness. You could raise the flowers in a candelabra or small pedestal container. As with an informal dinner, stand candles separately or include them in the arrangement, but ensure that they are long enough not to burn down before dinner ends.

EVERYDAY ARRANGEMENTS

Everyday flowers need to last well and the arrangement should not be too difficult to construct. Deep containers, wide, fairly deep bowls, containers with a slightly raised base and simple cylindrical vases or jugs are all ideal. The principles relating to table layout on pages 70–71 of this chapter are equally applicable for every day. With this in mind some ideas might include using a fairly deep container with a heavy pinholder in the base and containing a few flowers from the garden plus a small bunch from a florist, selected to pick up the colours in a table-cloth. The plant material needs to have

Flowers from the garden provide an informal, fresh touch for any meal. This tall arrangement is particularly suitable for a kitchen or similar table when not in use.

Flowers & foliage:

BLUE MONKSHOOD, KNAPWEED 'MOUNTAIN BLUE', YELLOW BLANKET FLOWER, YELLOW AND PEACH ACHILLEA, PALE YELLOW SCABIOUS, WHITE FEVERFEW, PURPLE LOOSESTRIFE, PINK SPIRAEA, WHITE OX-EYE DAISY, *WEIGELA FLORIDA VARIEGATA* FOLIAGE.

both different forms and textures and should vary slightly in size.

You could use a similar container or a lowish bowl for an arrangement comprising one type of flower such as daffodils (*Narcissus* spp.), anemones (*Anemone* spp.), roses or tulips (*Tulipa* hybrids) plus some leaves to help support the flowers and break up the slightly solid effect. A cap of

chicken wire over the pinholder helps to support the stems in a low, wide container. Since these containers hold plenty of water, the humidity produced will help prolong the life of the flowers. Very colourful or multi-patterned cloths are practical and attractive for every day, but a flower arrangement containing a similar number of colours would, of course, be lost on such a cloth. You would find it more effective to pick out one of the colours and arrange the flowers in tints, tones and shades of the chosen one. A fairly neutral container such as a low, rectangular oven dish, a pale green bowl or a circular container with a slightly raised base in a dull shade of green might complement both arrangement and cloth.

You could use a bowl for an arrangement of a few flowers such as daffodils, irises (*Iris* spp.),

roses or gerbera (*Gerbera* spp.) fixed on a pinholder. Place some large leaves at the base to hide the pinholder and provide visual weight.

Place tall arrangements at one end of the table, unless the table is not being used for dining. When using a glass container, support fine stems with thicker plant material; use florist's foam, pinholders or chicken wire to anchor plant material in non-transparent containers.

An everyday flower arrangement should not be too difficult to construct. This simple design uses different forms and textures to provide interest, and the deep container will not need frequent filling up.

Flowers & foliage:

PALE PINK TULIPS, BLUEBELLS, PURPLE LENTEN ROSE, MAUVE TULIPS, GREEN STINKING HELLEBORE FLOWERS, YELLOW DEAD NETTLE (LEAVES SPLASHED SILVER).

Mechanics: LARGE PINHOLDER.

THE KITCHEN

A SIMPLE CONTAINER OF FLOWERS is particularly apt in the kitchen, helping to make the working environment a more attractive place. Many kitchens have a breakfast bar, and what could be more uplifting than a few flowers in a small container for a bright start to the day? Larger kitchens may have space for a table, which is an ideal spot for a colourful display of flowers. Open any home-making magazine and you will find flower arrangements in most pictures of kitchens; these may be a mass of colourful tulips (*Tulipa* vars.) in a glass jug, pretty pink and white spray chrysanthemums (*Chrysanthemum* spp.), carnations (*Dianthus* spp.) and gypsophila (*Gypsophila paniculata*) in a shiny blue china jug, or yellow narcissus (*Narcissus* vars.) in a white cylindrical container. Every room is enhanced by an arrangement.

A simple but effective idea for an informal arrangement is to float flower heads in a shallow bowl of water.

Flowers & foliage:
PINK HYDRANGEA HEADS, HYDRANGEA LEAVES.

There are a number of basic considerations to bear in mind in the kitchen. All arrangements need to stand steadily. Additionally, the warmth of the kitchen means flowers need plenty of water both to weight the container and to provide humidity for the plant material.

Jugs in various forms are ideal containers, are easy to pick up by the handle to move them, and their large water capacity prevents the arrangements from drying out. Since they are designed to hold liquid, jugs should not leak and they should stand steadily. Plain or patterned vases in simple, uncomplicated shapes, unglazed pottery jugs or bowls and china or plastic plant pot holders are all ideal, as are many items of china, pottery or glass which you may find in your kitchen cupboards.

MECHANICS

Glass vases and jugs do not require any mechanics, but the flower stems should be clean with no leaves or surplus twigs under the water which would show through the glass. When placing the stems in the container ensure that they support one another so that they do not fall out; alternatively, you can bunch them and tie them lightly with wool before placing them in the container.

Lightly crumpled chicken wire can be used to support the stems in a non-transparent vase, and a pinholder used under the wire in a wide-necked vase or on its own if the stems are fairly

Brighten and soften any
working area like the
kitchen with a striking
one-colour arrangement.
The fluffy mimosa helps to
support the stems of the
tulips and daffodils.

Flowers & foliage:
YELLOW MIMOSA,
DOUBLE YELLOW TULIPS,
YELLOW NARCISSUS
'CHEERFULNESS'.

sturdy. It is not normally necessary to change the water in a container; all that is generally required is a filling up with some lukewarm water. Arrangements in transparent glass vases or jugs may, however, cause the water to become murky and unsightly before the flowers have died, particularly when using long-lasting flowers such as chrysanthemums. Empty out the water, clean the vase, refill with lukewarm water and return the flowers to the vase, re-cutting the stems if they appear dry.

TYPES OF ARRANGEMENTS

The warmth of the kitchen is ideal for forcing out spring blossoms such as yellow forsythia (*Forsythia* spp.), pink cherry and almond blossom (*Prunus* spp.) and purple, mauve and white lilac (*Syringa* spp.) which also provide a changing decoration during this process; once opened they can be arranged anywhere in the house. I remove any leaves, particularly those of lilac, and then condition the flowers by the boiling water treatment (*see* page 9).

A simple arrangement of one kind of flower can provide a vibrant splash of colour. Spray chrysanthemums, tulips or narcissi are ideal. You can cut the flower heads to the same level and then mass them into a container of suitable height and shape such as a globe, a straight-sided cylinder or square jar or a jug. This fairly expensive type of design can be made more economically with spring flowers, which can be purchased in inexpensive bunches. Alternatively you could float flower heads such as those of hydrangeas (*Hydrangea* spp.), lotus lilies, or water lilies (*Nymphaea* spp.) in a low bowl.

HERBS FOR FLOWER ARRANGEMENTS AND COOKING

There are many types of herbs which can be used for flower arranging either on their own or together with flowers. Their pleasant smell helps to perfume the air, you will have a leaf or two ready for your cooking and some herbs are said to deter flies and other insects.

Both herbs and flowers can be dried in the kitchen. Loosely packed bunches secured with an elastic band and string for hanging look most attractive when strung in the window or beneath a shelf. (The elastic band is necessary because the stems shrink as they dry and the bunch tends to

Hang herbs in bunches in the kitchen for their pleasant aroma. They will dry and can be used for cooking. The simple arrangement in a pottery jug and raffia plait with dried flowers complement one another well. Many herbs can be used for both culinary and floral aids.

Flowers & foliage:
PINK HONEYSUCKLE, YELLOW ACHILLEA, YELLOW LOOSESTRIFE, BLUE BRODIAEA, BLUE PERENNIAL GERANIUM, VARIEGATED GERANIUM, IVY, SCENTED GERANIUM LEAVES; TANSY LEAVES.

HANGING HERBS: RUE, CHIVE FLOWERS, TARRAGON, SAGE, MINT, GOLDEN LEMON BALM.

fall apart if secured by string only.) Flowers suitable for drying are listed in the Directory of Flowers and Foliage on pages 46–51.

Small plants thrive on a kitchen windowsill or in a window box provided they are well fed and watered. Herbs with variegated or coloured foliage or pretty flowers such as golden lemon balm (*Melissa officinalis*), purple sage (*Salvia officinalis* 'Purpurascens') or lavender (*Lavandula* spp.) make handsome additions to a herbaceous border. Choose a sunny corner of the garden for a collection of herbs and place flat stones at the front of the border (low creeping plants will soon fill the spaces and the stepping stones will enable

you to reach the rear of the border). A raised bed in the corner of a patio with containers of varying heights in front of the bed is a particularly good place to grow herbs; as well as being easily accessible the herbs provide a fragrant addition to the sitting area of the garden.

Generally, herbs thrive in sunny conditions and are not difficult to grow, but some herbs need a little extra care. Rosemary (*Rosmarinus officinalis*) needs protection from the wind and tall herbs such as fennel should be planted at the back of the border and staked. All forms of mint tend to spread rapidly and may need to be restrained in some way.

HERBS FOR ARRANGING AND COOKING

The following is a list of some useful herbs with suggestions for flower arrangements and which foods they best complement.

Bay (Lauraceae)
● *Evergreen aromatic tree. Can grow to 23 feet (7 metres). Slow growing. Can be trimmed for a small garden and put in tubs for a patio.*
● *Decorative evergreen foliage, long sprays for pedestal arrangements. Can also be used in smaller arrangements as elliptical leaf is about 2 inches (5 cm) long.*
● *Use in bouquet garni, marinades, as infusion for sauces – one leaf is sufficient as bay has strong flavour when fresh.*

Fennel (Foeniculum vulgare)
● *A 5 foot (150 cm) tall perennial plant with thick stems and fine green feathery leaves. Dainty yellow umbels of flowers are borne in late summer. Seed heads can be preserved in glycerine. Bronze fennel has deep bronze leaves; a handsome, tall plant.*
● *The tall, fine flowers add a lacy texture to designs.*
● *The aniseed flavour of the chopped leaves is good with oily fish, pork or lamb.*

Lemon balm (Melissa officinalis)
● *A 2 foot (60 cm) tall perennial with rounded, wrinkled soft green leaves with a lemon scent. The small white flowers are insignificant. Aurea variety has leaves splashed with gold.*
● *The tall spikes of leaves last well in arrangements, the golden varieties being particularly attractive.*
● *Lemon-scented leaves can be used with fish, poultry and salads; they also make a tonic herbal tea.*

Mint (Mentha spp.)
The many varieties are perennials which grow to a height of 18 inches (45 cm). Leaves usually green.
● *All mints are useful in flower arranging. Apple mint has leaves edged in white and buddleia mint has pale grey green downy leaves and 2 inch (5 cm) pointed flowers.*
● *Many culinary uses depending on flavour. Common mint is delicious with lamb and peppermint makes a tasty herbal tea.*

Curry plant, or white-leaf everlasting (Helichrysum angustfolium)
● *Perennial shrub with spiky silver 'evergreen' leaves; height 18 inches (45 cm) to 2 feet (60 cm).*
● *Sprays of fine silvery leaves most attractive in small traditional designs. Do not use as part of dinner table arrangement as curry smell is very pervasive.*
● *Chopped leaves can be added to stuffings and sauces for a mild curry flavour.*

Sage (Salvia)
● *Evergreen shrub with rough-textured, grey-green leaves, up to 2 feet (60 cm) in height. Purple sage and variegated sages have attractively coloured leaves.*
● *Interesting aromatic leaves, particularly the variegated and purple varieties.*
● *Use in bouquet garni, in stuffings for pork and duck, sprigs with cooked vegetables. Use also for sage teas and for hair rinses.*

Marjoram (Origanum onites)
● *An 18 inch (45 cm) high perennial which forms a neat mound spreading annually. Has small green leaves and tiny heads of pink, white or mauve flowers. The golden variety is very attractive.*
● *The sprays of tiny leaves are ideal for petite arrangements.*
● *A fairly strong flavour for marinades, stuffings and pasta dishes; the leaves can also be used for a soothing herbal tea.*

Rosemary (Rosmarinus officinalis)
● *Evergreen shrub which can grow to 6 feet (180 cm) tall. The spiky grey-green leaves are aromatic and the pale blue flowers appear in the spring.*
● *The spikes of grey-green leaves last well; useful as outline material.*
● *Good flavour when sprigs are inserted in roast lamb, pork or chicken. Chopped leaves can be added to stuffings. Rosemary tea makes a rinse for dark hair.*

BEDROOMS
AND BATHROOMS

A FLOWER ARRANGEMENT in your guest's bedroom is a welcoming touch and helps to make your friends feel at home. Remember to look after the flowers and to replace them as necessary during any guests' visits, as nothing is worse than a neglected arrangement which may give the impression that your friends have outstayed their welcome.

Do not forget your own bedroom; a simple posy or even an elegant rose (*Rosa* spp.) in a stem vase helps to cheer the beginning and end of each day.

Bathrooms can also be brightened with flowers; these can be fresh or more permanent arrangements of dainty dried flowers. Very often plants that will not thrive anywhere else in the house flourish in the humid atmosphere of the bathroom.

This loose arrangement with its gentle pink and white colour scheme harmonizes with the soft, restful atmosphere of the bedroom. The weighty container on the chest is unlikely to be knocked over.

Flowers & foliage:
PALE PINK ROSES, PINK PAEONIES, PALE AND DUSKY PINK SPRAY CARNATIONS, DEEP PINK SEA LAVENDER, SNOWBALL BUSH FLOWERS AND FOLIAGE, *COTONEASTER FRANCHETII.*

Mechanics: HEAVY PINHOLDER, NYLON JERSEY MATERIAL, FLORIST'S FOAM, TAPE.

A trio of roses in a stem vase echoes the design of the mirror frame and, reflected in the mirror, gives double the amount of colour. The glass vase has a heavy base to prevent it tipping over.

Flowers & foliage:
DEEP PINK ROSES.

BEDROOM ARRANGEMENTS

Generally, there is not a great deal of room for flower arrangements in a bedroom, consequently the designs need to be fairly small. Having said this there are, of course, exceptions. You can make charming arrangements in a jug and basin on an antique wash-stand and a pretty design in a deep bowl on a small, round table.

Petite arrangements of less than 9 inches (23 cm) in overall measurement are in the main best for a dressing-table which is usually cluttered with bottles of perfume, jars of make-up, brushes and combs, photographs and other paraphernalia. Little designs need to stand very steadily on a solid and heavy base as the dressing-table is the workplace of the bedroom. The same criteria apply both to arrangements on the bedside table and larger arrangements generally and care must be taken that the flowers are not knocked over in the dark. On a mantelpiece, one or two roses or other choice flowers placed in a stem vase look most attractive; remember, though, that these vases do not hold very much water, so the level should be checked every day.

A group of tiny arrangements in small containers such as a silver box or a porcelain jug can look charming on an occasional table beside framed photographs of loved ones. They also look pretty on shelves amongst *objets d'art*.

The beauty of small garden flowers or evergreen leaves shows to advantage in these designs, whereas their small scale might be lost in larger arrangements. Soft-stemmed flowers such as primroses (*Primula* spp.), violets (*Viola* spp.), anemones (*Anemone* spp.), grape hyacinths (*Muscari* spp.) and love-in-a-mist (*Nigella damascena*) will last for several days in a cool bedroom. Small rockery plants, miniature roses, side sprays of delphiniums and larkspur (*Delphinium* spp.), tiny flowers from shrubs like the tamarisk (*Tamarix* spp.), oleander (*Nerium oleander*), heather or ling (*Calluna vulgaris*) and hebe (*Hebe* spp.) all look delightful arranged with a few sprigs of foliage in a little container.

Another idea is to use any small flowers remaining from a large arrangement. One stem of gypsophila, mimosa, or silver wattle, (*Acacia dealbata*) or a Michaelmas daisy (*Aster* spp.) provides dainty filling material and heather or asparagus ferns (*Asparagus plumosus*) or eucalyptus (*Eucalyptus* spp.) have small leaves for petite arrangements or use a few house-plant leaves. Sweet-scented geraniums (*Pelargonium* spp.), tradescantia (*Tradescantia fluminersis*), small ferns, kangaroo vine (*Cissus antarctica*) and the Busy Lizzie or Patient Lucy (*Impatiens holstii*) all have small foliage. They also last a long time in water and may well form roots for later repotting.

83

MECHANICS FOR SMALL ARRANGEMENTS

Many tiny designs require no mechanics other than a container full of water. You can place small sprays of leaves, a few sprays of heather, gypsophila or mimosa in the water first to support the fragile flowers which you add later. An alternative is to make a pretty bunch in your hand, tie it with soft wool, cut the stem ends to the same length and place the posy in the

Some welcoming ideas for a bedroom. The posy arrangements make good use of small garden flowers. The colours of all the arrangements reflect the general colour scheme of the room.

Flowers & foliage:

POSIES: MIXED SWEET WILLIAM, ANEMONES, PALE MAUVE LILAC, PINK SWEET PEAS, GREY-GREEN *SENECIO LAXIFOLIUS* 'SUNSHINE', EUONYMUS 'EMERALD AND GOLD', VARIEGATED CANARY ISLAND IVY.

LARGE ARRANGEMENT: PALE MAUVE SINGLE LILAC, DARK PURPLE DOUBLE LILAC, MAUVE STOCKS, PINK/RED/WHITE SWEET WILLIAMS, PINK FREESIAS, SWEET PEAS, PAEONY LEAVES, PHYSOCARPUS LEAVES, FLOWERING CURRANT LEAVES.

84

container. This method is particularly suitable for bunches of primroses or violets surrounded by a frill of their own leaves. A small block of soaked green florist's foam can be used to support more sturdy stems, and for dried arrangements dry foam is suitable.

CONTAINERS FOR SMALL ARRANGEMENTS

Tiny wicker baskets are very popular and they are available in many shapes, with or without handles or lids. Silver cigarette boxes, tea caddies, patch boxes and small silver bowls as well as egg cups, small glass vases, wine glasses and coloured glass jars make ideal containers. Many famous firms which produce china dinner services also make sets of prettily decorated *objets d'art*; these collections usually include a vase which is suitable for an arrangement of a few small flowers.

DRIED FLOWERS

Dried flowers are convenient for the bedroom, particularly on a bedside table where water could spill out of a vase of fresh flowers. Alternatively, they can be made into plaques, pictures, hanging balls of flowers and swags to add a splash of colour and visual interest to the walls.

Many true everlasting flowers are dainty enough for small designs. The everlasting daisies or immortelles have papery or straw-like petals or bracts; they dry well if cut before they are fully open. Different varieties are the sand flower (*Ammobium*), strawflower (*Helichrysum bracteatum*), sunrays (*Helipterums*) and *Xeranthemum*. Statice (*Limonium* [*statice*] spp.) is known as sea lavender, so-called because of the pointed shape of the clusters of little flowers. The pearly everlasting (*Anaphalis* spp.) has clusters of tiny white daisy flowers and silver-grey foliage. For methods of drying flowers, *see* pages 14–15.

THE SCENTS OF SUMMER

What could be more delightful than a room lightly perfumed with fragrant flowers, herbs and spices. Pot-pourri, sachets and cushions all provide scent for the room, inside cupboards and drawers and on bed-linen. Simply pick sweet-smelling flowers and herbs from your garden, or if you do not have a garden, grow aromatic herbs in pots on the kitchen windowsill. Any perfumed flowers will provide suitable material.

Mechanics: FOAM HOLDER, FLORIST'S FOAM, TAPE.

POT-POURRI

Any scented plants can be used to make pot-pourri; it is, however, the judicious blending of the flowers, herbs, fruits, barks and spices that produces the subtle aroma. Select a main, strong scent such as rose, lavender flowers or lemon verbena leaves before adding other perfumes for complementary undertones. A few drops of essential oil will strengthen the perfume, but use it with restraint so as not to mask the other delicate perfumes. Attar of roses is most commonly used and sandalwood, bitter almond, peppermint and clove are other oils; all may be purchased from a herbalist or pharmacist.

You can experiment with different scents and blendings until you find a combination which gives you pleasure. The choice of scented plant material is vast: consider roses, lilac, lily of the valley, oleander, jasmine and orange blossom. Herbs have scented leaves, but some are too powerful for a pot-pourri; the various mints, lemon balm, rosemary and the scented geraniums are worth trying.

Spices such as allspice, nutmeg, cinnamon, aniseed and cloves add an exciting aroma to the pot-pourri and dried citrus peel gives a tangy scent.

Finally, the pot-pourri will require a fixative to hold the perfume; orris root, available from pharmacists or herbalists, is ideal for this purpose.

MAKING THE POT-POURRI

Roses and lavender retain their scent particularly well and form the basis of most pot-pourris.

The amounts given are measured after drying.
4 cups rose petals
1 cup lavender flowers
1 cup rosemary flowers and leaves
½ cup jasmine
½ cup pinks
1 cup scented leaves, such as lemon verbena, scented geranium or sweet marjoram
⅓ cup orris root powder
3 tsp mixed spices
Few drops of your chosen essential oil

Collect the plant material on a dry day after the dew has dried on the petals and leaves, then spread them out on a rack or a tray and set to dry in a warm, dark, airy place. Larger flowers such as roses should have their petals removed in order to dry them separately. The plant material will take about 10 days to dry; it should then be mixed with the rest of the ingredients and stored in a sealed container in the dark for about 6 weeks. Shake or stir the mixture daily so that the various perfumes blend together. The pot-pourri can then be placed into pretty china, glass or metal bowls or some other suitable container. When the perfume fades it can be rejuvenated with one or two drops of the essential oils.

HERB PILLOWS AND SACHETS

Herb pillows and little sachets which can be hung in the cupboard or placed in drawers give a light perfume to a bedroom. The cushions and sachets should be constructed from a fine, pretty material, strong enough not to let the contents escape yet with a loose enough weave to allow the perfume to escape. Fill with a light pot-pourri mixture or with soothing combinations of herbs.

A sweet-smelling pillow which helps prevent headaches can be made from 1 part dried sweet marjoram, 2 parts dried lavender flowers, 6 parts dried lemon verbena and a few crushed cloves. Fleas on dogs and cats can be discouraged with a pillow consisting of 1 part dried rue and 1 part dried rosemary.

CITRUS POMANDERS

Pomanders were carried during the Middle Ages as they were thought to ward off the plague and other pestilential diseases. Today they are made to perfume drawers or, hung on a ribbon, they look decorative in the bedroom.

To make a pomander, select an unblemished orange, lime, lemon or other small citrus fruit. Section the fruit into quarters with narrow pieces of sticky tape, then prick the fruit with a needle, inserting a clove into each hole. A small space can be left between the cloves to allow for shrinkage of the fruit. Roll the pomander in a few mixed spices and orris root to fix the perfume. Remove tape and tie a length of pretty ribbon in the resulting space. Place the pomander in a paper bag and set it to dry in an airing cupboard; it will shrink and become quite hard, retaining its scent for years. The pomander may be decorated with a few dried or artificial flowers.

THE BATHROOM

The bathroom is an ideal place for a sweet-scented posy of flowers or perhaps a small group of house-plants which grow well in the steamy atmosphere. Many ferns, particularly the maidenhair fern, grow well in the bathroom, especially when grouped together in a bowl.

CONTAINERS

As in the bedroom, containers need to be stable, particularly since the flowers may be placed on a narrow shelf. If space allows, a jug and bowl make a most attractive container. For smaller spaces you could use pretty soap dishes or shells, or containers in the shape of a fish. When using shells for fresh flowers make sure that they are waterproof. If not, they can, of course, be used for an arrangement of dried flowers.

Arrangements of colourful dried flowers provide a more permanent display for the bathroom. Care should, however, be taken not to place them where the steam rises as they will then wilt and may become covered with mildew.

Try to complement the décor with your flowers and containers; you could even include an accessory such as a classical alabaster figurine for a cool and elegant effect.

Above: make sure that shell containers are steady, non-porous and have sufficient water capacity for your flowers. The cling film- (plastic wrap) wrapped foam helps to prevent the escape of moisture. The succulents last well out of water.

Flowers & foliage:
PINK SWEET PEAS AND ALSTROEMERIA, PALE YELLOW FREESIAS AND STATICE, GREY-GREEN BALLOTA, SILVERY- GREY CURRY PLANT (WHITE-LEAF EVERLASTING), JAPANESE ANEMONE, SUCCULENTS.

Mechanics: FLORIST'S FOAM WRAPPED IN CLINGFILM (PLASTIC WRAP).

Right: this pretty and
informal bathroom
arrangement uses an old
basin and ewer for its
containers.

Flowers & foliage:
BLUE DELPHINIUMS,
YELLOW LABURNUM,
MAUVE STOCKS, MAUVE
LILAC, KNAPWEED
'MOUNTAIN BLUE'.

Mechanics: HEAVY
PINHOLDER, CHICKEN
WIRE.

THE
GARDEN ROOM

BOTH A CONSERVATORY AND A GARDEN ROOM are very versatile additions to traditional living space, and they can be made most attractive with groups of green and flowering plants and one or two flower arrangements.

Although the garden room is usually full of plants, it is very pleasant to introduce some colour in the form of a flower arrangement. Baskets made of natural plant material, pottery jugs or bowls and wooden containers are all suitable for this setting. The arrangement could stand on a table or chair or be hung from the wall or a hook fixed in the ceiling. Lightweight baskets require heavy dishes or a weighty

pinholder to prevent the basket from tipping over. A stone figurine or bust makes an attractive accessory for your garden room designs, and shells, coral or rocks add interest and a different texture.

The conservatory is often more of a workplace than the garden room; it may be used as a greenhouse for tender plants, for growing young plants from seeds and cuttings and for the display

of house-plants, including samples which may be too large for the house. Its function will vary depending on whether or not it is heated.

A garden room differs from a conservatory in that it is a part of the garden and, although enclosed, its glass walls permit a view of the lawns and flower borders. It is an ideal place in which to sit on a sunny day in winter or it can provide shelter on a windy day. A garden room can become very hot in summer, so good ventilation and blinds to filter the sunlight are essential. You can decorate the room with house-plants, tubs or hanging baskets full of colourful annual flowers, with tender climbing plants such as passion-flower (*Passiflora* spp.), jasmine (*Jasminum polyanthum*) or flamboyant bougainvillea (*Bougainvillea* spp.). Simple arrangements of garden flowers or a *pot et fleur* also look attractive in the garden room.

Far left: the stone bust to the right of this simple arrangement makes an attractive accessory for a garden room. As with all accessories place it in position before you begin the arrangement.

Flowers & foliage:
PALE MAUVE COLUMBINE, CHAMPAGNE ROSES, DOUBLE WHITE RANUNCULUS, CREAM ANEMONES WITH MAUVE AND PINK CENTRES.

Left: freshly-picked flowers in a wicker basket bring a little of your garden inside. Place a heavy pottery bowl in the basket before assembling the mechanics, flowers and foliage in the bowl.

Flowers & foliage:
SOLOMON'S SEAL FLOWERS AND LEAVES, CREAM MEXICAN ORANGE BLOSSOM, DOUBLE PURPLE LILAC, BLUE CALIFORNIAN LILAC, LIME GREEN *EUPHORBIA ROBBIAE*, PURPLE BERBERIS FOLIAGE, GOLDEN PHILADELPHUS, MEXICAN ORANGE BLOSSOM FOLIAGE.

Mechanics: HEAVY PINHOLDER, NYLON JERSEY MATERIAL, FLORIST'S FOAM, CHICKEN WIRE, TAPE.

During the winter-time these glass rooms can become very cold unless they have some form of heating; this should be considered when planning your arrangements. In the summer time the rooms may become very hot and, unless the glass walls and roof are shaded, the leaves and flowers may dry out very quickly and become scorched. You will need adequate ventilation to keep down the temperature and to prevent the atmosphere from becoming too humid, which can cause mould to form on the plants.

To be able to grow plants out of season, such as many flowering bulbs, tender plants like mimosa, or silver wattle (*Acacia dealbata*) and plumbago (*Plumbago capensis*) and house-plants from hot countries is a special bonus to the flower arranger. All varieties of succulents grow well in garden rooms. Their intricate shapes make attractive additions to arrangements and they last a long time out of water.

You can grow flowers for cutting in the conservatory or garden room. Stocks (*Matthiola* spp.), carnations (*Dianthus* spp.), scented and variegated geraniums (*Pelargonium* spp.), camellias (*Camellia* spp.), lilies (*Lilium* spp.) and orchids such as *Cymbidium* spp., *Bletilla striata* or *Pleione* spp. are just a few of the many varieties which flourish.

POT ET FLEURS AND HOUSE-PLANTS

A *pot et fleur* is very attractive in a conservatory or garden room and can be made following the instructions opposite.

A handsome group of house-plants gives a much more satisfying and dramatic effect than a single plant on its own. Sometimes just two or three plants grouped together give a touch of colour where it is needed. A few flowering plants look much more impressive when they are combined with foliage plants.

Plants thrive when they are placed together, generally benefiting from the humid atmosphere. It is also much quicker to water a group of plants than single ones located in different parts of the house. You can either replant them in a single shared container or group them near each other at different heights in a decorative container. The whole effect is most harmonious when the containers are similar in style.

WHAT YOU WILL NEED

Flowers & foliage: SEVEN CREAM GERBERAS, PARADISE PALM, CREEPING FIG, VARIEGATED DUMB CANE, RIBBON FERN, MAIDENHAIR FERN, VARIEGATED IVY.

Other materials: GREEN CERAMIC BOWL 13 INCHES (33 CM) WIDE AND 5 INCHES (13 CM) DEEP, GRAVEL OR SMALL PEBBLES, A FEW PIECES OF CHARCOAL, POTTING SOIL, SMALL FLAT-BASED PLASTIC CONTAINER ABOUT 3 INCHES (8 CM) DEEP AND 4 INCHES (10 CM) WIDE, 3-INCH (8-CM) PINHOLDER AND FLORIST'S FIXING CLAY (A WELL PINHOLDER MAY BE USED), TROWEL.

1 *place layer of gravel in the base of bowl plus a few pieces of charcoal (these assist drainage and keep the soil sweet). Fix pinholder in plastic container and place in centre of bowl. Remove tallest plant from its pot and position at centre back of bowl, spreading out roots a little.*

2 *remove remaining plants from pots and position in bowl with larger plants towards back. Some plants may need to be angled to flow attractively over edge of the bowl.*

3 *fill gaps between plants with potting soil (at room heat), leaving about 1/2 inch (1.25 cm) between top of soil and rim of bowl to allow sufficient space for watering. Re-cut gerbera stems, then add gerbera in a vertical stepped line through centre, pressing stems firmly into pinholder.*

The finishing touch: *stand bowl on a table in conservatory. Fill plastic dish of flowers with lukewarm water, then water plants and spray with water. NOTE: The cream gerbera flowers need to be conditioned by the boiling water treatment and given a 24-hour drink in deep water before using.*

POT ET FLEUR

STAGE **1**   STAGE **2**   STAGE **3**

GIFTS AND SPECIAL OCCASIONS

*T*HERE IS NOTHING MORE DELIGHTFUL than to receive a gift of flowers from your loved ones or a friend. A pretty posy of flowers and leaves from the garden, a selection of flowers from the florist, a formal arrangement of flowers or a group of pot plants and flowers in a bowl make pleasantly personal gifts.

Parties or other special occasions can be enhanced by flower arrangements which evoke a particular atmosphere or a theme. As always, the flowers should welcome your guests and may well provide an additional talking point. Whenever you are planning a party the overall effect needs to be considered. Generally, one or two large arrangements have more impact than several smaller ones scattered around the room. Some occasions call for a particular colour scheme: red or gold for ruby or golden wedding anniversaries, blue or pink for a baby boy's or girl's christening or red for Saint Valentine's Day are just a few examples. Remember that the flowers should complement the existing furnishings and choose colours carefully.

This Saint Valentine's Day arrangement derives its impact from the dramatic red roses lightened by the yellow freesias and foliage.

Flowers & foliage: DEEP RED ROSES, PALE YELLOW DOUBLE FREESIAS, SCARLET SPRAY CARNATION, EUONYMUS 'SILVER QUEEN', LONOKI CYPRESS *'CRIPSII'*, COMMON IVY 'GOLD HEART'.

Mechanics: FLORIST'S FOAM.

This colourful posy in a basket would make an ideal present for someone in hospital. It is easily portable and has a wide base to help prevent it from being knocked over.

Flowers & foliage: PINK AND GREEN *ASTRANTIA MAJOR*, BLUE LOVE-IN-A-MIST, PINK ALSTROEMERIA, WHITE PHLOX BUDS, EUONYMUS 'EMERALD AND GOLD', ROSEMARY FOLIAGE, PHYSOCARPUS.

Mechanics: PLASTIC FOAM HOLDER IN A SMALL PLASTIC DISH PLACED IN THE BASKET, FLORIST'S FOAM.

FLOWERS FOR GIFTS

Arrangements which need to be transported should be firmly secured to ensure that the arrangement does not collapse in transit. Secure mechanics as you would for large arrangements – *see* page 12.

FOR FRIENDS IN HOSPITAL

A friend in hospital will certainly appreciate an arrangement which you have created yourself, and you can arrange the flowers attractively at home in a container. A completed arrangement also saves the busy nurses' time. There are many inexpensive containers which are suitable for a hospital bedside locker. The main criterion is that they have sufficiently wide bases so that they do not get knocked over easily. Baskets with an inner container, small plastic bowls and plastic containers with a short stem are all ideal. There should also be sufficient space for water between the foam and the edge of the container. Do not fill the container to the top with water until it is *in situ*, otherwise water will probably spill out on the way to the hospital.

SELECTING THE FLOWERS

Both flowers and foliage should be long-lasting and very well conditioned. The patient may appreciate an arrangement from his or her own garden and will most certainly enjoy a selection of favourite flowers in a favourite colour. Avoid flowers of a dark yellow shade, or those with jarring or very bright colours or a strong perfume, and concentrate on pretty, lightly perfumed flowers such as freesia (*Freesia* spp.), carnations (*Dianthus* spp.) or chrysanthemums (*Chrysanthemum* spp.).

If you are unable to transport a completed arrangement of flowers, an attractive posy is a possible alternative: remove the lower leaves, then group the flowers and leaves in your hand, changing their positions until the arrangement pleases you. Tie the stems together with a piece of knitting wool; when you have cut the stems a matching ribbon can be tied over the wool to hide it. Cut the stem ends to the same length, and place in a plastic bag for transport. Remember to re-cut the stem ends before placing the posy in a vase of water.

93

MOTHER'S DAY GIFT

STAGE **1**

STAGE **2**

STAGE **3**

1 *secure foam holder into centre of container with florist's fixing clay. Cut a square block of foam large enough to fit inside container and to protrude about 1½ inches (4 cm) above edge of hamper. This is necessary so that stems may be inserted into the side of the block for a downward, flowing movement. Soak foam in water until fully charged, then press it on to foam holder. Tape foam securely in container. Define basic outlines of arrangement with flowering currant, add hosta leaves to strengthen centre, begin filling in with euonymus.*

2 *add some buds of spray carnations at outer edges and more open flowers towards centre. Continue triangular shape, first with bluebells, then with chrysanthemums, keeping largest, most open flowers in centre. Recess a few spray carnations in the centre and fill in centre and back with shorter pieces of flowering currant.*

3 *add tulips in a stepped vertical line through the centre, cutting soft stems straight across to insert into foam. Add a few sprays of spiraea 'gold flame', to repeat some of the flower colours.*

The finishing touch: *add yellow mimosa for a different texture, to fill out arrangement and conceal foam. Fix cream bow to front of hamper. Fill container with water.*

MOTHER'S DAY

Mother's Day or Mothering Sunday is the traditional day on which children give gifts of flowers to their mothers to thank them for all their loving care. A mother might be given breakfast in bed on this special day, and a few pretty flowers in a little glass vase to brighten up the breakfast tray would be well received.

Posies are an attractive way to present flowers on Mother's Day. They can be made in the way described above or in the form of a tussie mussie or Victorian posy.

Tussie mussies are little nosegays. Made up of sweet-smelling flowers and whole dried herbs, they keep their scent for a long time. They were carried until the eighteenth century by all manner of people because their perfume disguised the noxious smells of the streets and they were thought to be protect the carrier from infection. Any herbs or fragrant flowers can be used to make a tussie mussie.

Victorian posies are made in a similar way but use more colourful circles of flowers placed close together. They may be finished off with a frill of lace or paper and ribbon streamers. Alternatively a harmonious arrangement of green and flowering house-plants in a bowl decorated with a ribbon bow makes an attractive and long-lasting gift.

Another idea is to place the gift in a box such as a shoe box and then decorate the top with a small arrangement of dried or silk flowers. Wrap the lid and bottom of the box separately in giftwrap, cut a small block of dry foam and wrap it in fine string netting, then fix it to the lid of the box with two stub wires pushed through the lid and twisted at the back. Complete your arrangement, place the gift in the box and seal the lid with transparent sticky tape.

HOW TO MAKE A TUSSIE MUSSIE

1 *begin with a small flower like a rose bud.*

2 *surround this with feathery leaves of rue and rosemary and tie the bunch with wool.*

3 *continue with two or three different herbs, finishing off with a circle of more solid-looking leaves such as lemon balm or geranium.*

4 *tie the nosegay tightly.*

Roses, pink tulips, carnations and champagne glasses with ribbons around their stems, on a silver tray, make a luxurious celebratory arrangement. The silver container is lined with a plastic bowl to avoid any scratching from the flowers and foliage.

Flowers & foliage:
CHAMPAGNE ROSES, WHITE GYPSOPHILA, VERY PALE PINK TULIPS, PINK SPRAY CARNATIONS, PALE MAUVE HEATHER, BLUE-GREEN WESTERN HEMLOCK, VARIEGATED SILVER-GREY SCENTED GERANIUM LEAVES.

Mechanics: PLASTIC FOAM HOLDER IN A PLASTIC DISH, FLORIST'S FOAM.

SPECIAL OCCASIONS

Apart from Mother's Day, there are many other special occasions such as a birthday or summer party, and weddings, each of which will require different types of floral decoration.

On Saint Valentine's Day a single rose displayed in a stem vase is always appreciated, while heart-shaped vases or containers and red flowers and ribbons would convey the theme to guests at a Saint Valentine Day's party.

A BIRTHDAY BUFFET PARTY

Any birthday party should incorporate the favourite flowers and colours of the birthday person but should also take into account the table setting colours.

Sturdy pedestal arrangements placed against the wall or a bold display on the mantelpiece or on top of a bookcase would show up well at a party. Alternatively you could remove a picture – where practical – and put a hanging arrangement of fresh or dried flowers in the party colours in its place or decorate branching wall lights with ribbon streamers and a small swag or posy of artificial or dried flowers. The buffet table on which the food is displayed might include a tall, stemmed container with a candle in the centre of the arrangement and further candles in tall candlesticks to provide a soft, romantic light to an evening party. A birthday cake, which will have pride of place on the table, can be given even more prominence with asymmetric arrangements in toning colours placed on either side of it. It could also be raised on a stand encircled by a wreath frame filled with dainty flowers and foliage (*see* page 111).

If space allows, a fairly large interpretative arrangement could form the centrepiece. This should, of course, complement the person who is celebrating a birthday and perhaps reflect one of their interests. A landscape design with driftwood, ferns, grasses and simple flowers shows a love of the countryside; two Dresden figures linked by an archway of trailing foliage and surrounded by dainty flowers might suit a collector of fine porcelain. For someone who loves a particular sport, just a glimpse of a team scarf with flowers picking out the colours would be sufficient for a design. Small records on sticks, black painted swirling driftwood and brightly coloured flowers might interpret a young person's love of contemporary dancing. Another idea is to use the birthday person's star sign as the central theme. For instance, 'Pisces' might suggest a marine theme with fishing nets, shells and flowers matching the colours of the sea.

Guests may be seated at various tables around the room and in other parts of the house and arrangements in small bowls or a sturdy wine glass might echo the overall colour scheme and add a festive touch. Even if the guests do not use these tables, keep the surfaces fairly clear of glasses, plates, ashtrays and so on, and design arrangements which are not too large.

OTHER PARTS OF THE HOUSE

A co-ordinating colour scheme throughout the house gives a unified effect; it is also less expensive to buy flowers in tints, tones and shades of one colour for the whole house. Since your guests will enter the house through the front door they will notice a welcoming arrangement in the hall at once before they move to other parts of the house. A small posy in the cloakroom and even a simple arrangement in a shell in the bathroom are attractive touches.

An unusual idea for a birthday party using the same flower design for the cake and table arrangements, and linking them with pink ribbons.

Flowers & foliage:
DORIS PINKS, PALE PINK SPRAY CARNATIONS, WHITE FEVERFEW, GREEN LADY'S MANTLE, FORSYTHIA, VARIEGATED PERIWINKLE, HONOKI CYPRESS 'CRIPSII'.

Mechanics: PLASTIC FOAM HOLDER, FLORIST'S FOAM, CANDLE HOLDERS, SMALL PLASTIC DISHES ON CAKE, JAM JAR LID.

Opposite: make afternoon tea a special occasion with a tiered arrangement. This one is framed by the toning yellow flowers in the background.

Flowers & foliage:
YELLOW AND PINK POLYANTHUS ROSES, BLUE CORNFLOWERS, PALE BLUE BRODIAEA, GOLDEN ROD, YELLOW AND WHITE PAINTED DAISY, *WEIGELA FLORIDA VARIEGATA*, JAPANESE ANEMONE.

Mechanics: FLORIST'S FOAM SHAPED TO FIT INTO THE TIERED, PAINTED METAL CONTAINER.

SUMMER PARTIES

Entertaining in the garden provides a refreshing and totally different vista to indoor parties in naturally delightful surroundings.

During the day the flowers and foliage in the garden will form a backdrop for your flower arrangements. When planning, decide where they will be placed and then consider the colour scheme in the garden and the cloths, napkins and candles you intend to use.

There are some specific problems about arranging flowers for al fresco parties. During the day the sun can be very hot, so tough plant material which does not wilt easily should be chosen. It is a good idea to choose a shady spot for your arrangement – perhaps under a garden parasol. If there is a light breeze or even a wind, your arrangements will need steady bases and plenty of water as they transpire quickly in the sun and wind. A heavy vase with flowers cut low and arranged in water helps overcome this problem. Alternatively, use a deep bowl containing a block of florist's foam with a cap of 2 inch (5 cm) chicken wire securely taped to the sides of the bowl. Tall, stemmed containers are not recommended as they may topple over in the wind or on an uneven surface.

A Byzantine cone of flowers is useful for using up all the short-stemmed flowers which may be left over from the other arrangements. The bases of these cones may be made several days in advance, saving time on the day of the party. The cones are very simple to make (*see below*).

Summer parties in the evening will probably take place in fairly subdued lighting, sometimes in candle-light. Consequently the flowers will need to be light coloured and luminous to show up well. Always enclose the candles for an outdoor party in glass-sided lanterns or candle holders with a glass chimney so that they are safe and do not continually blow out.

HOW TO MAKE A BYZANTINE CONE

1 use a low container with a short stem and a soaked block of foam shaped into a rough cone.

2 fix the foam on to a heavy foam holder secured in the container.

3 cover it with bushy small-leafed foliage such as box.

4 add flowers with short, firm stems and small fruits fixed on to cocktail sticks (toothpicks).

Flowers for outdoor summer parties can be simple and informal; choose them to tie in with a theme or setting.

Flowers & foliage:
WHITE TRUMPET LILY.

Church pew arrangements for a wedding should be colour co-ordinated to complement the bridesmaids' dresses and bride's bouquet.

Flowers & foliage: PALE YELLOW ROSES, FREESIA AND SPRAY CARNATIONS, LEMON YELLOW SPRAY CARNATIONS, CREAM SINGAPORE ORCHIDS, HONOKI CYPRESS *'CRIPSII'*, *COTONEASTER FRANCHETII*, IVY LEAVES.

Mechanics: FLORIST'S FOAM IN A SPECIAL CONTAINER FOR HANGING ARRANGEMENTS.

WEDDING FLOWERS

It is a great honour to be asked to arrange flowers for a wedding, whether for a member of your own family or for a friend. The wedding photographs and perhaps a video film will be treasured for many years and the flowers often feature prominently in these mementoes of the day.

A wedding is the bride's special day and her wishes should be your first consideration when planning the decorations. Nevertheless, as the flower arranger you should be able to advise and guide the bride and her mother when necessary. Many people have no idea about how much flowers cost, so it is useful to know the approximate cost of each different arrangement. These may include a pedestal arrangement, a design for the buffet, arrangements in a candelabra, a tiny vase for the top of the cake, pew ends, swags and garlands for the church or marquee (tent). You will need to work out numbers and types of flowers for each

arrangement; visit the florist or wholesaler to check the current cost of the flowers. With this information at your fingertips you will be able to advise both bride and mother so they can then work out how many arrangements they can afford. If you are arranging the flowers for a friend and they wish to give you some form of remuneration, then add a certain amount to the cost of each arrangement. If you are not very experienced, arranging the flowers will probably take you quite a long time, in which case payment by the hour would not be practicable.

The next consideration should be the overall colour scheme of the wedding. This is usually set by the colour of the bridesmaid's dresses, assuming the bride is traditionally dressed in white or cream. Whether the scheme is taken from the dress of the bride or those of the bridesmaids it is helpful to have a piece of the dress material in order to select the right shade, texture and type of flowers. The scheme looks most harmonious with some flowers matching the exact shade of the dresses, and with the remaining flowers in tints and tones of this colour. White and cream come in different shades, so try to find just the right shade. Sometimes the main colour is fairly strong: the bridesmaids' dresses and the walls of the marquee (tent) might both be deep coral. Coral flowers would not show up against these walls, so lighter colours such as peach and cream would be preferable with perhaps a touch of coral running through the centre. The table arrangements might include a little pale mauve for contrast. Do beware, however, of using mauve or blue when an arrangement is to be viewed from a distance, as they tend to recede, so that all you will see are dark spaces and not the flowers.

The principal colour can be used for ribbon bows and streamers to hang below pedestal arrangements or swags attached to the marquee (tent) poles and pew ends. Ribbons can save you money by taking the place of a few flowers.

THE CHURCH

Flower arrangements should complement the architecture of the church and help to create a special atmosphere. Before deciding on the position of any decorations contact the vicar and the person in charge of the church flowers. They should be able to tell you where to find vases, equipment and helpers. Some churches do not allow flowers on the altar or in the font, and during Lent and Advent some churches do not allow flowers at all.

Remember that churches can be fairly dark places, even with the lights switched on. Select positions which are well lit by natural or artificial lighting whenever possible. You will find that light-coloured luminous flowers will show up best.

A fairly tall arrangement placed near the entrance will welcome people as they walk into the church. If practicable, the font makes an ideal container. Swags on the pew ends always look lovely, but ensure that they do not impede the progress of the bride up the aisle. A pedestal arrangement by the chancel steps, one by the altar, and arrangements on windowsills, around the pulpit and on the table where the register is signed are probably sufficient. Remember that arrangements on the altar will be seen from a distance, so they need a clean outline, should be lower than the cross and preferably curve towards it. Avoid the temptation to cover every flat surface with an arrangement; a few bold designs have much more impact.

Outside the church, arrangements on the porch seats, tubs of flowering plants or topiary trees set the wedding scene. The latter are simple to construct and look most effective.

A church window arrangement needs to be seen from a distance.

Flowers & foliage:
WHITE GLADIOLI, YELLOW TIGER LILY, YELLOW ROSES AND SPRAY CARNATIONS, YELLOW SPIDER CHRYSANTHEMUMS, WHITE MOCK ORANGE BLOSSOM, WHITE DOUBLE BELLFLOWER, WHITE SPRAY CARNATIONS, JAPANESE ANEMONE FOLIAGE, FORSYTHIA FOLIAGE, *COTONEASTER FRANCHETII*, LADY FERNS.

Mechanics: FLORIST'S FOAM, CHICKEN WIRE, TAPE, DEEP BOWL.

HOW TO MAKE A TOPIARY TREE

1 cut a length of 1 inch (2.5 cm) dowelling to the required length.

2 sink it into a painted plastic flowerpot filled with plaster of Paris and allow this to set.

3 screw a plastic bowl-shaped container to the top and place a block of chicken wire in the container, taping down securely.

4 form an even shape with evergreen foliage such as box or cupressus.

5 dot flowers such as carnations or daisy chrysanthemums throughout the design.

6 finish with a ribbon bow and streamers hanging under the arrangement.

7 ribbon can be wound around the stem or it can be painted to match the flowerpot and container.

Positioning the reception arrangements

Your next action will be to decide where you are going to place all the flower arrangements. If the reception is to take place in the house, the colour scheme should continue throughout the house. (*See* the section on birthday flowers on pages 96–97 for suggestions.)

For a reception in a marquee (tent) or dining hall you will need to have a plan of the layout of the tables and the position where the bridal party will be receiving their guests. The cake usually has a small arrangement on the top with fresh or artificial flowers in the chosen colour scheme for the wedding.

The cake may be placed on a separate small table; this would look pretty with looped garlands around the edge or with a lace overcloth caught up on each side with a small swag of flowers and ribbon streamers hanging down to the floor. Decorate the top table similarly.

Pedestal arrangements need a very steady base when used out of doors or in a marquee (tent). A heavy column or an urn on a plinth are less likely to fall over on uneven ground or in the crush of guests. A pedestal beside the receiving line looks attractive as do two or three more set against the walls. Long, low arrangements on the top table enable the bridal party to see and be seen. The shape of the other tables will decide the shape of the arrangement: round for round tables and long and low for rectangular ones.

You might decorate the walls of the marquee (tent) with ribbon bows and streamers on the wall lights and swags or arrangements in semicircular wire hanging baskets. You can wind fresh garlands around the poles of the marquee (tent) or fix three or four large swags around the poles well above head height.

HOW TO MAKE A SWAG

1 soak a block of florist's foam in water, then wrap first in thin plastic sheeting and then in 2 inch (5 cm) chicken wire.

2 hammer two 4 inch (10 cm) nails into pole.

3 either put the block of foam onto the nails and arrange the flowers in situ, or arrange them flat on a table and, when completed, fix the foam and flowers to the nails.

4 check that no foam shows at the sides and then tie the swag onto the pole for extra security.

SPECIFIC PLAN OF ACTION

For most weddings and receptions in a church and marquee (tent), you will need at least two helpers and it will probably take all day.

Having decided on the colour scheme, work out the type and number of flowers required for each arrangement, the foliage which you will need and whether it can be picked from the garden or must be purchased from the florist. Order the flowers at least two weeks in advance; your florist should be able to advise you about availability.

Flowers & foliage:
PINK PAEONIES, PINK STATICE, CHAMPAGNE ROSES, PEACH AND WHITE SINGAPORE ORCHIDS, WHITE AND PINK NANUS GLADIOLI, CREAM LILIES, CARNATIONS AND GLADIOLI, LADDER FERN, VARIEGATED CANARY ISLAND IVY, EUONYMUS 'SILVER QUEEN', VARIEGATED PERIWINKLE FOLIAGE, SUMMER JASMINE TRAILS, VARIEGATED NORWAY MAPLE.

Mechanics: A WREATH FRAME IN TWO HALVES WITH FLORIST'S FOAM INSIDE, RE-JOINED.

Far left: the general colour scheme of pedestal arrangements should take into account the colour of the marquee (tent) walls and colour theme of the wedding.

Flowers & foliage:
AS ABOVE BUT *MINUS* CREAM LILIES, CARNATIONS, SUMMER JASMINE, VARIEGATED NORWAY MAPLE.

Mechanics: FLORIST'S FOAM, CHICKEN WIRE, TAPE, DEEP PLASTIC BOWL, STONE CONTAINER.

Ensure you have sufficient buckets for all the flowers and foliage, florist's foam, containers, chicken wire, florist's tape and ribbon.

Two days before the wedding, collect and condition flowers and bought foliage, pick and condition garden foliage, soak the foam and prepare containers. Insert long-lasting greenery into swags, pew ends, small table arrangements and topiary trees and make ribbon bows.

On the day before the wedding, pack the flowers and foliage into flower boxes or buckets, keeping the material for each arrangement separate as it will save time later. Transport all that you need to the first venue: this is usually the church as it is the coolest place. A plastic sheet spread on the floor protects the surface and enables you to work tidily. When you have finished, fill the containers with water. Leave the decorations for outside the church inside overnight. In frost they will turn black.

On the day of the wedding take a little extra foliage with you in case any has flopped; carefully fill up the containers with water and finally place the outside decorations in position.

SEASONAL
CELEBRATIONS

THROUGHOUT THE YEAR there are many traditional national and international occasions to celebrate with a party. New Year is one such occasion; all the Christmas decorations remain until 12 days after Christmas but you might like to add to them for the New Year. A special centrepiece on a buffet table might interpret the Old and the New Year with lichened driftwood and glycerined leaves to represent the year past, and spring flowers to herald the year to come. Progressing through the year, the next major celebratory time is Easter, followed by the American fourth of July festivities and Independence Day, then Hallowe'en, Thanksgiving and Harvest Time.

Another way of presenting spring flowers in a basket. The straight, upward lines of the tallest plant material and the strong, mixed colours create a dramatic effect.

Flowers & foliage:

YELLOW AND PINK
TULIPS, YELLOW
FORSYTHIA, RED AND
YELLOW TULIPS, DARK
BLUE AND WHITE IRIS,
WHITE TULIPS, PINK
GERALDTON WAX PLANT,
FASCIATED WILLOW,
WHITE HYACINTHS,
GREEN EUPHORBIA,
GOLDEN PRIVET.

Mechanics:

PINHOLDER, NYLON
JERSEY MATERIAL,
FLORIST'S FOAM, CHICKEN
WIRE, TAPE, HEAVY
POTTERY BOWL INSIDE
THE BASKET.

EASTER

*E*ASTER IS A TIME when many people remember the suffering and the Resurrection of Christ – a new beginning in a new year. The beautiful white arum, or calla, lilies with which many churches are decorated at this time seem to convey the feeling of new birth in their pure white form. Yellow and white narcissus (*Narcissus* hybrids), blue irises (*Iris* spp.), primroses (*Primula* spp.), hyacinths (*Hyacinthus* spp.) and branches of blossom are the real harbingers of spring.

Spring flowers do not have the longevity of those produced later in the season, but their fleeting beauty gives immense pleasure. Daffodils (*Narcissus* hybrids), irises, tulips (*Tulipa* hybrids) and anemones (*Anemone* spp.) are best purchased in bud with just a touch of colour showing.

Blossom such as forsythia (*Forsythia* spp.) or prunus (*Prunus* spp.) can be forced out early in the year. Cut the sprays on a frost-free day, give them a drink in hot water and leave in a warm place. The buds can be encouraged to open by spraying them occasionally with warm water.

Pussy willow and twigs covered in dancing catkins will give height to arrangements of smaller spring flowers, and the newly emerging Italian arum (*Arum italicum pictum*) leaves give weight and form an interesting base.

Baskets make particularly attractive containers for spring flowers as they are made of natural plant material, and the woven twigs, cane or rushes can be duplicated in the flower arrangement. They come in many shapes and sizes from those with a handle to picnic hampers and nest-like baskets.

Easter and spring flowers are synonymous. Coupled with a basket container and Easter eggs, this arrangement epitomizes the revival of life in the new season.

Flowers & foliage: PALE BLUE PERIWINKLE FLOWERS AND VARIEGATED FOLIAGE, PALE BLUE IRIS AND HYACINTHS, PINK FLOWERING CURRANT FLOWERS AND FOLIAGE, PINK HONEYSUCKLE AND FOLIAGE, PINK AND WHITE *VIBURNUM TINUS*, CONTORTED WILLOW TWIGS, ITALIAN ARUM LEAVES.

Mechanics: 3 METAL FOAM HOLDERS, FLORIST'S FOAM IN A SHALLOW PLASTIC DISH THAT FITS IN THE BASKET CONTAINER.

NATIONAL FESTIVALS

During these festivals either the national flower or the flag of the country is the centrepoint. National colours tend to be bright, such as red, white and blue for the American flag. An arrangement to celebrate a national day might include the national flowers and one or two colours from the flag with the third colour used for the base, accessory or ribbons.

HALLOWE'EN

H ALLOWE'EN FALLS ON THE EVE of All Saints' Day, 31st October. On this night witches are supposed to fly through the sky on their broomsticks accompanied by their black cats, silhouetted against the moon. They were supposed to be guided by Jack o' Lanterns with twinkling, mysterious lights.

Exciting, dramatic designs help to create the eerie atmosphere of Hallowe'en. Flaming red and orange flowers and grasses, colourful fruits, weird, twisting black wood, seed heads and red reedmace, bulrushes, or cattails, (*Typha* spp.), to represent fireworks all arranged on a black base or in a 'witches' cauldron' would set the scene for a Hallowe'en party. The witches can be kept at bay with candles inside hollowed-out pumpkins (squashes) or swedes (rutabagas) with goblin faces cut in the sides.

This is an exciting evening for children and, if the weather is kind, you could hold the party outside with the light provided by the candles in the pumpkins and a firework display to enliven the festivities.

The eerie atmosphere of Hallowe'en can be created using all manner of designs. The use of brightly coloured flowers and different textures under flickering candlelight can create all sorts of visual effects. Most of the dried material here is available from florists.

Flowers & foliage:
SCARLET GERBERA, RED APPLES, DRIED FUNGI, LOTUS SEED HEADS SPRAYED GOLD, CHIPPED FAN PALM, SCORCHED TEASLES, RED BULRUSHES (CATTAILS), FLAME TREE PODS, AFRICAN SEED HEADS AND PINK AND ORANGE GRASS SILK TASSEL BUSH AND *MAHONIA JAPONICA* LEAVES, PURPLE SMOKE BUSH (EUROPEAN BEECH) FOLIAGE.

HARVEST TIME
AND THANKSGIVING

*T*HE GATHERING IN of the harvest and
thankfulness for its abundance takes place
in the autumn of the year.

HARVEST TIME

In Britain the Harvest Festival occurs at any time
in October or November. It is mainly a time for
celebrating in churches and chapels followed by
the traditional harvest supper held in church halls
and barns. Special loaves of bread are baked by
the local baker for the Harvest Festival services
and are often given pride of place on the church
altar. You could include small loaves, fruit and
vegetables in an arrangement on a wide
windowsill, while on the opposite side placing
grapes, old wine bottles and red wine-coloured
flowers to interpret the harvesting of the vines. A
pedestal arrangement might include fresh
sweetcorn (maize) and apples on sticks, fresh and
glycerined leaves, preserved seed heads, colourful
autumn chrysanthemums (*Chrysanthemum* spp.),
dahlias (*Dahlia* spp.) and berries. Pampas grass
(*Cortaderia* spp.) can be used to give height to the
arrangement and several ears of wheat (*Triticum*
spp.) will emphasize the harvest theme.

*Bright autumn
chrysanthemums,
glycerined and dried leaves
and seed heads make this
pedestal arrangement ideal
for a traditional harvest
supper. Always use plant
material in good condition
when preserving and avoid
both young leaves and
those which have already
turned colour, when
preserving by the glycerine
method.*

Flowers & foliage:
YELLOW APPLES, YELLOW
SWEETCORN, YELLOW

SPRAY
CHRYSANTHEMUMS,
YELLOW GLADIOLI, DRIED
YELLOW ACHILLEA, DRIED
SCOTCH THISTLE SEED
HEADS, DRIED
SWEETCORN, PHEASANT
FEATHERS, GLYCERINED
BEECH, RUSCUS,
ASPIDISTRA, EUCALYPTUS,
LAUREL, BRACKEN,
MAGNOLIA GRANDIFLORA,
ALEXANDRIAN LAUREL.

Mechanics: FLORIST'S
FOAM, CHICKEN WIRE,
TAPE, DEEP BOWL,
PEDESTAL.

You could use similar pedestal arrangements in the hall for the harvest supper plus a centrepiece for the buffet table which may include fruit and flowers flowing out of a basket. You could co-ordinate all of the arrangements with large swags of autumn foliage, flowers, berries and seed heads, which would provide a splash of colour against the plain walls. (To make swags *see* page 102.)

THANKSGIVING

Thanksgiving, on the fourth Thursday of November (the second Monday in October in Canada), is a time in America when families gather together to remember the early settlers' happiness. It is the time of year when the settlers were thankful for their first successful harvests.

The theme of the floral decorations is similar to that of the British Harvest Festival, but in this case the home is usually the setting for the celebration. Whether the family gathering is large or small, your flower arrangements should show the abundance of harvest in rich, glowing autumn colours. Maize (corn), wheat, exotic fruits and nuts can all be incorporated into the designs. Baskets make most suitable containers and accessories as their natural colours blend well with that of the autumnal plant material. Basketware cornucopias or horns of plenty are appropriate for a display on a buffet table.

Simple candles will light the scene with a mellow glow and will echo the celebrations of the early settlers, who also used candle-light.

Above: an arrangement for a Thanksgiving dinner table in rich autumn colours, which reflects the abundance of the harvest and takes into account the tableware.

Flowers & foliage: DRIED CORN, DRIED HARE'S TAIL GRASS, YELLOW APPLES, PURPLE GRAPES, PECAN NUTS, WALNUTS, BABY SWEETCORN, PEACH SPRAY CHRYSANTHEMUM, VARIEGATED CANARY ISLAND IVY, GLYCERINED BEECH AND ALEXANDRIAN LAUREL.

Mechanics: FOAM HOLDER, FLORIST'S FOAM, TAPE, SMALL PLASTIC DISHES INSIDE THE BASKET CORNUCOPIAS.

CHRISTMAS

*F*OR THOUSANDS OF YEARS before the birth of Christ there were pagan festivals to celebrate the passing of midwinter. It was a time of goodwill, when dwellings were decorated with evergreens, including holly, ivy and branches of fir. Gifts were exchanged in honour of various gods, and the god Odin was especially honoured in northern Europe with small gifts hung on the fir trees. The evergreens were revered because their leaves and fruits remained on the trees during the long winter.

The true date of Christ's birth was not known and so the newly established Christian Church celebrated His birth at the time of year when the pagans celebrated the promise of the renewal of life in the year to come.

Today we delight in decorating our homes and churches at Christmas with the traditional evergreens, and the fir tree which was decked with gifts in honour of Odin is now our Christmas tree.

PLANNING AHEAD

The few weeks before Christmas can be a very busy time, so some advance planning will mean that you are less rushed and can enjoy preparing the decorations at your leisure.

You can start in July by preserving sprays of leaves in glycerine for use in their natural state (*see* page 14) or covering them with gold or copper paint. In midsummer look out both for interesting seed heads which can be dried as well as fir cones and teazles (*Dipsacus* spp.).

Well before Christmas decide on your theme. You might want traditional evergreens with touches of red, white and gold, or a silver, white and glittery theme, or perhaps less traditional decorations which complement the style and décor of your house. Whatever your choice, remember that shops stock up earlier and earlier for Christmas and in order to find the best selection you will need to visit them in November or even late October.

At the beginning of December pick berried holly (*Ilex* spp.), otherwise the birds will eat the berries, especially during a hard winter. While some people suggest that the branches can be laid on the grass under sacking or plastic, I prefer to stand the sprays in water in a cool place.

Artificial and preserved decorations can be made at any time during December and stored until Christmas Eve. Arrangements using sturdy evergreens and fresh or artificial flowers can be prepared at least a week before Christmas. Store these in a cool place and add the fresh flowers on the day before they are needed.

TOOLS AND EQUIPMENT

Gather all your tools and equipment together in a shallow box or on a tray to enable you to move them easily from place to place. You will probably need the following:
● sharp scissors, secateurs (pruning shears), craft knife and wire cutters
● stub, fine and reel wires
● spray paint and glitter
● glue, sticky tape, florist's tape, stem binding tape, cocktail sticks (toothpicks), kebab sticks
● round or square cake boards to use as bases. If a special shape is required, take a paper pattern to a local D-I-Y store and they will cut the board for you.
● ribbon, both satin and flock finish, plus special ribbon for outside
● silk-covered balls and other baubles

THE DECORATIONS

A few larger decorations are more effective than several smaller ones scattered throughout the house, and an overall theme is more practical and economical. Concentrate your decorations in four main areas: the front door, hallway, living-room and dining-room.

As it is very expensive and time-consuming to create decorations almost entirely of fresh plant material, you will find it more practical to combine fresh, preserved and artificial material.

WIRING A CONE

1 push one end of a length of heavy-gauge stub wire through lowest band of scales, leaving 2 inches (5 cm) jutting out.

2 wind wire tightly into cone, then twist ends together to grip cone.

3 bend ends under cone and trim short end. Wind gutta-percha tape around long stem wire to conceal.

TRADITIONAL CHRISTMAS WREATH

WHAT YOU WILL NEED

Flowers & foliage: VARIEGATED BOX, CUPRESSUS, VARIEGATED HOLLY, IVY, DRIED SEA LAVENDER, APPLES, CEDAR AND CANADIAN SPRUCE CONES.

Other materials: RING OF FLORIST'S FOAM, TURNTABLE, WOODEN KEBAB STICKS, STUB WIRE, STRONG STRING, WATERPROOF FLOCK RIBBON.

This festive wreath is created in the following way:

1 *soak the ring of florist's foam and place on turntable. Add sprigs of box and cupressus to inside and outside edges.*

2 *add variegated holly for interest. Fill in with ivy and cupressus.*

3 *position sprays of dried sea lavender at regular intervals. Break wooden kebab sticks in half, push into apples and then into foam. Insert wired cedar cones at bottom of wreath.*

The finishing touch: *use strong string to tie wreath to door. Add wired Canadian spruce cones, then tie a waterproof flock ribbon to one side to soften outline of cones.*

| STAGE *1* | STAGE *2* | STAGE *3* |

Some decorations which can be prepared in advance and assembled later:

1 place glycerined leaves, cones and seed heads outside on several sheets of newspaper and lightly cover with copper or gold paint. Alternatively, complete the preserved part of an arrangement, lightly paint, allow to dry, then add any further material such as artificial flowers or baubles.

2 glitter painted leaves when wet by placing the glitter and leaves in a large plastic bag and shaking it lightly. Paint fresh leaves with glue and glitter in the same way.

3 lengthen wire cones and artificial leaf sprays, if necessary, on kebab sticks.

4 decide on the colour scheme for your dining-table and buy candles, matching napkins and cloths. Select candles at least 10 inches (25 cm) tall; they are far more elegant than shorter ones and take longer to burn down. Ensure you have a plentiful supply as they may be required on several occasions. Tape cocktail stick (toothpick) 'legs' to candles for use in arrangements.

5 pick and condition long-lasting foliage before inserting it into swags (*see* page 102), cones (*see* page 98), wreaths (*see* page 111) and topiary trees (*see* page 101).

THE CHRISTMAS TREE

Order your Christmas tree from a reputable supplier. If the tree has no roots, saw a slice off the bottom and place the tree in a bucket containing fertilizer. Spray the leaves with water every day before planting in damp sand or soil and transferring the tree to the house. If the tree has roots on, re-cut any dry ends and proceed as before. Continue to water the tree, but do ensure the inner container has drainage holes.

A Christmas swag for an inglenook or above a fireplace is a dramatic and colourful way of acknowledging this all-important festival.

Flowers & foliage:
IN HEARTH: VARIEGATED HOLLY 'GOLDEN KING', WILD IVY AND CONES.

SWAG: HIMALAYAN PINE AND ORIENTAL SPRUCE CONES, CUPRESSUS FOLIAGE.

Mechanics: SMALL BLOCKS OF FLORIST'S FOAM ENCASED IN CLING-FILM (PLASTIC WRAP) AND TIED WITH STRING IN BETWEEN EACH BLOCK.

CHRISTMAS FLOWER ARRANGEMENTS

Red, white, gold and green are the traditional and favourite colours for Christmas arrangements. Bright red can be garish in rooms decorated in subtle colours, so white and gold might be a better choice here. Artificial plant material and baubles can be used to great effect, either alone or mixed with fresh or preserved material.

Remember that Christmas arrangements are the same shape and conform to the same elements and principles as those during the rest of the year; it is the material used that is slightly different. Some ideas might include welcoming your family and guests with a ribbon-decorated wreath or swag on the front door, or setting the scene in the hallway with a woodland scene of lanterns, driftwood, evergreens, Christmas roses (*Helleborus niger*) and robins.

Select long-lasting material for a warm living-room such as evergreens, carnations (*Dianthus* spp.) or chrysanthemums (*Chrysanthemum* spp.) and artificial or preserved material, or perhaps a *pot et fleur* including some red flowers (*see* page 57). You might want to paint large fir cones or a bunch of smaller ones with a mixture of essential oils such as sandalwood, orange or rose, then allow them to dry and hang them near a warm place to release the fragrance. Single cones on coloured ribbons would make an attractive and inexpensive tree decoration.

The decorations in the dining-room need to look just right both by day and in the evening.

Artificial arrangements, which can be made a week or so in advance, leave you free to enjoy Christmas festivities as the day approaches. Flowers can be made a week ahead, holly picked at the beginning of the month and the cones and seed heads collected in midsummer for drying.

Flowers & foliage: WAXED ARTIFICIAL CHRISTMAS ROSES, GOLD-SPRAYED COLUMBINE SEED HEADS, GOLD-SPRAYED CONES, VARIEGATED HOLLY, MEDITERRANEAN CYPRESS.

Mechanics: FOAM HOLDER, FLORIST'S FOAM, TAPE, STEMMED BOWL AND BASE COVERED IN DARK GREEN DUPION.

CONCLUSION

*I*HOPE THAT THIS BOOK has inspired you to create some beautiful arrangements for yourself and that you will gradually evolve your own particular style to suit the décor of your own home and your way of life.

Once you have learned the basic concepts and practicalities the scope is endless. I hope also that the use and association of different plant materials illustrated throughout this book will encourage you both to search out and grow some plants specifically for arranging.

It is a good idea to record your arrangements by taking a photograph of them; this will help to remind you of the materials you used and you will also be surprised to see how much your arranging improves over the months. You might find further inspiration in other people's ideas, by watching a skilled demonstrator, or by going to exhibitions or competitions. Why not join a flower or garden club or attend some classes in flower arranging?

From a simple vase of flowers in the kitchen to complex arrangements for weddings and other special occasions you should now be able to tackle almost any arrangement and feel thoroughly at home with flowers.

INDEX

Numerals in *italics* refer to illustrations.

ACKNOWLEDGMENTS

Swallow Books would like to thank the following people and organizations who have kindly assisted in the production of this book. We apologize to anyone we may have omitted to mention.

Olga Arathoon; Dr and Mrs B. Batten; Mrs Jill Bayly; Doris Beasley; Mrs Gwen Bowles; the Church of Saint Mary the Virgin, Strethall; Mr and Mrs J. Cordle; Mr and Mrs P. Creagh-Coen; Mr and Mrs D. Cummins; Mr and Mrs A. Duffas; Squadron Leader and Mrs C. Gillow; Mrs Joan Golfar; Mrs Norma Hall; Helen Harrison; Nicholas Hasler; Malcolm Higgins; Mr and Mrs D. Hill; Ed Hill; Mr and Mrs G. Jeffreys; Mrs Joyce Kingsman; Mary McNeil; Mr and Mrs S. Miller; Alan Morris; Mrs Maggie Motion; Elaine Partington; Mrs Mary Reardon; Brian Rusby; Mrs Val Simmonds; Mr and Mrs R. Thomas; Catherine Tilley; Air Commodore and Mrs D. Trotman; Mrs Mary Tucker; Stuart Wilsdon.

Flowers were supplied by:
Mrs Doris Brown, Salisbury; Hedley-Coombes, Salisbury; Mortimers, Salisbury; Paula Pryke Flowers, London.

Photographic props were supplied by:
Golfar and Hughes, London; Josiah Wedgwood & Sons Limited, London; Oggetti, London; Osborne and Little, London; Paula Pryke Flowers, London; Plasterworks, London.

Photographs:
Michael Holford (22); National Gallery London (71).

With thanks also to David Band and Kay Hinwood whose screen print and painting are in the photographs on pages 37 and 15 respectively.